Personal Best

Workbook

A2 Elementary

Series Editor
Jim Scrivener

Author
Genevieve White

1	You and me	p2
2	Work and play	p8
3	People in my life	p14
4	Home and away	p20
5	What are you wearing?	p26
6	Homes and cities	p32
7	Food and drink	p38
8	In the past	p44
9	Education, education!	p50
10	People	p56
11	On the move	p62
12	Enjoy yourself	p68
	WRITING PRACTICE	p74

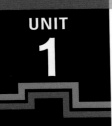

UNIT 1

You and me

GRAMMAR: The verb *be*

1 Choose the correct options to complete the sentences.

1 I *am / is / are* nineteen years old.
2 She *am / is / are* a teacher.
3 *Am / Is / Are* you from this country?
4 They *am not / isn't / aren't* at home.
5 We *am / is / are* all in the same class.
6 *Am / Is / Are* she English?
7 I *'m not / isn't / aren't* hungry.
8 It *am / is / are* nice to meet you.

2 Complete the sentences with the correct form of the verb *be*.

1 'Where's Malu?' 'I don't know. She _____ here.'
2 'Are you twenty?' 'No, I _____ twenty-two.'
3 My parents _____ in New York this week.
4 'Is Pablo your brother?' 'No. He _____ my friend.'
5 'Where are the children?' 'They _____ at home. They're at school.'
6 '_____ we all here?' 'No, James is in the classroom.'
7 You _____ a teacher. You're a student.
8 '_____ she Russian?' 'No, she's Polish.'

VOCABULARY: Countries and nationalities and numbers 1–1,000

3 Write the words or numbers.

1 95 _____
2 twenty-one _____
3 47 _____
4 two thousand _____
5 12 _____
6 six hundred and thirty _____
7 802 _____
8 eighty-five _____
9 13 _____
10 fifteen _____

4 Match flags a–f with nationalities 1–6.

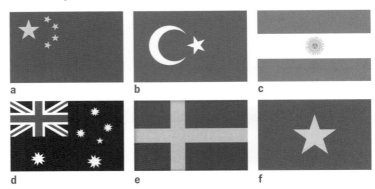

1 Swedish _____
2 Chinese _____
3 Australian _____
4 Argentinian _____
5 Vietnamese _____
6 Turkish _____

5 Complete the sentences with countries or nationalities.

1 My mum's from Japan. She's _____.
2 Our teacher is from _____. She's Canadian.
3 I'm from Ireland. I'm _____.
4 His best friend is from _____. She's Italian.
5 Marta is from Portugal. She's _____.
6 My dad's from the USA. He's _____.
7 They are _____. They're from Wales.
8 We are from Spain. We're _____.
9 Michel's _____. He's from France.
10 Wahid is from Egypt. He's _____.

PRONUNCIATION: Contractions of *be*

6 ▶1.1 <u>Underline</u> the contractions. Say the sentences. Listen, check and repeat.

1 'Are you eighteen years old?' 'No, I'm twenty.'
2 'Where is Miguel?' 'He's in a meeting.'
3 This is the café. We're eating breakfast here.
4 Anna is my sister. She's an English teacher.
5 They're my friends. We are in the same class.
6 I know you. You're Sasha's brother.
7 'Is your car German?' 'No, it's Italian.'

SKILLS 1B

READING: Approaching a text

My trip with the orchestra

Hi! I'm Paola and I'm from Portugal. I ¹_____ a student, but I'm also in a guitar orchestra for young people. At the moment, I'm on a trip with the orchestra. We're ready to play concerts in London, Paris and Rome! Here's my blog about my month of music.

WEEK 1

These are some of my friends from the orchestra. They ²_____ great fun! Maria ³_____ nineteen and Miguel is eighteen. They're my best friends. We usually go to the park together – we all like nature. We're in London at the moment, and there are lots of beautiful parks here.

WEEK 2

Our guitar teacher's name is Carlos and he's very friendly. He is a great teacher – and he also cooks dinner for us every night. We all like his food very much.

WEEK 3

We ⁴_____ in Paris now, in a hotel near the city centre. There are a lot of English students in this hotel, so I practise my English every day. The orchestra plays music every morning until midday, and then we walk around the city. It's a really interesting place and we see and do lots of things.

WEEK 4

We're in Rome now. It ⁵_____ an exciting city! Our concerts ⁶_____ in the evening, and we go shopping every day. My month of music is nearly finished. I'm happy because I want to see my family, but I'm sad because this trip is great.

1 Look at the title, headings and pictures. Choose the best description for the text.
  a Someone who goes to music school every day.
  b Someone who travels with her orchestra for four weeks.
  c Someone who visits Rome in the holidays.

2 Complete the text with the correct forms of the verb *be*.

3 Are the sentences true (T), false (F) or doesn't say (DS)?
  1 Paola is Portuguese. _____
  2 Her friend Maria is Spanish. _____
  3 There are nice parks in London. _____
  4 Carlos is a bad cook. _____
  5 There are no French students in the hotel in Paris. _____
  6 Miguel doesn't like Paris. _____
  7 Paola likes Rome. _____
  8 Maria and Miguel like shopping in Rome. _____

3

1C LANGUAGE

GRAMMAR: Possessive adjectives and 's for possession

1 Choose the correct options to complete the sentences.

1 My classmates and I all like ___ English teacher.
   a our   b his   c their
2 'What is your ___ name?' 'Her name's Giulia.'
   a sisters   b sisters'   c sister's
3 'Is this ___ key?' 'Yes – it's mine.'
   a my   b your   c her
4 Do you like ___ shoes? They're new!
   a Jame's   b James   c James'
5 'Where does Enrico live?' '___ house is over there.'
   a Its   b His   c Your
6 'Is Emma at home?' 'No. Her ___ car isn't here.'
   a parents   b parent's   c parents'
7 I have a white cat. ___ name is Snowy.
   a My   b Their   c Its
8 This shop doesn't have ___ bags.
   a womens   b women's   c womens'

2 Complete the text with possessive adjectives.

Juan

I'm Juan and this is a photo of ¹_____ class. You can see my best friend – ²_____ name's Marta – and ³_____ teacher. ⁴_____ name is Pedro and he has two children. ⁵_____ names are Luisa and Carlos.

This is a photo of my house. Mum and I live here. It's a small house, but ⁶_____ garden is quite big – we both like gardening! We have a cat, too – ⁷_____ name is Sooty because it is black and white. What about you? What are ⁸_____ friends and house like?

VOCABULARY: Personal objects

3 Match definitions 1–6 with objects a–f.

1 You can see your face in this. ___
2 You open a door with this. ___
3 You can talk to your friends with it. ___
4 You wear these on your hands when it's cold. ___
5 You need this when it rains. ___
6 You put your money in it. ___

a umbrella
b purse
c phone
d gloves
e key
f mirror

4 Complete the words.

1 This is a p ___ ___ ___ ___ of me with my mum and my sister. We are on holiday!
2 You can buy a s ___ ___ ___ ___ for your postcard at the post office.
3 What's the time? I don't have a w ___ ___ ___ ___.
4 When I walk at night, I take a t ___ ___ ___ ___ to help me see.
5 My name and address are on my i ___ ___ ___ ___ ___ ___ ___ c ___ ___ ___.
6 I eat a lot of s ___ ___ ___ ___. My mum says they're bad for my teeth.
7 I can't read this without my g ___ ___ ___ ___ ___ ___.
8 We can't eat c ___ ___ ___ ___ ___ g ___ ___ in lessons.

PRONUNCIATION: Sentence stress

5 ▶ 1.2 Listen and repeat the sentences. Underline the stressed words in each sentence. Listen again, check and repeat.

1 What's in his wallet?
2 Here are your books.
3 My tablet is on the chair.
4 What's her name?
5 Their house is new.
6 Where are my tissues?

SKILLS | 1D

SPEAKING: Asking for and giving personal information

1 ▶1.3 Listen to the conversation. Which sentence is correct?

A Miguel is at home.
B Miguel is on the phone.
C Miguel is at the gym.

2 ▶1.3 Listen again. Complete the sentences.

1 What's your f_____ name?
2 And what's your _____?
3 Do you have an _____ address, Miguel?
4 And what's your _____ number, please?
5 What's your a_____?
6 OK. What's your p_____?

3 ▶1.3 Listen again and complete the form below.

4 ▶1.3 Does the receptionist ask for clarification for Miguel's information? Listen again and write A, B or C for 1–6.

A Yes, she asks 'How do you spell that (please)?'
B Yes, she asks Miguel to repeat information.
C No, she doesn't ask for clarification.

1 first name ____
2 surname ____
3 email address ____
4 phone number ____
5 address ____
6 postcode ____

5 ▶1.4 Look at the information in the form below. Listen and check if it is correct. Ask for clarification and make sure you use polite intonation.

SUPERFIT GYM Date:

CLIENT INFORMATION

First name:

Surname:

CONTACT DETAILS

Email:
@starmail.com

Phone number:
077

Address:
30 Road

Postcode:

SUPERFIT GYM Date:

CLIENT INFORMATION

First name:
MARIA

Surname:
PALMA

CONTACT DETAILS

Email:
palma90@newmail.co.uk

Phone number:
07700990816

Address:
13 Broughton Road

Postcode:
EH5 7AZ

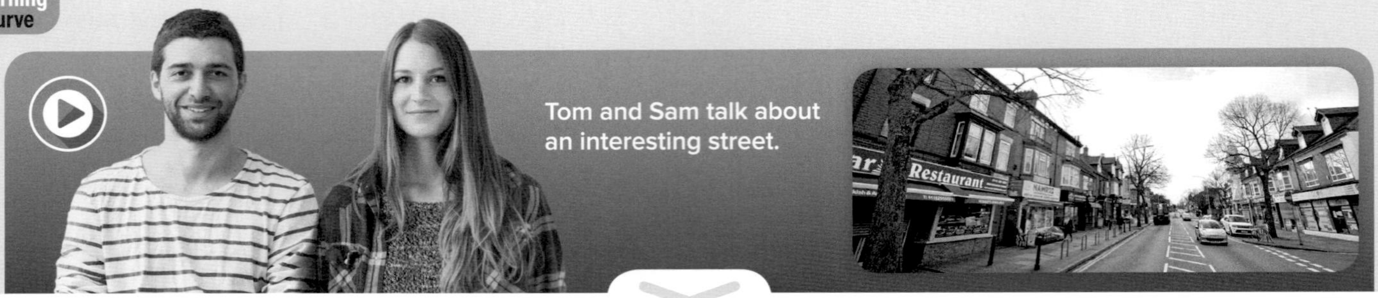

1 REVIEW and PRACTICE

HOME BLOG **PODCASTS** ABOUT CONTACT

Learning Curve

Tom and Sam talk about an interesting street.

LISTENING

1 ▶ 1.5 Listen to the podcast about an interesting street. Read the sentences. Are they true (T) or false (F)?

1 Narborough Road is in the UK. _____
2 It's interesting because it's a very international street. _____
3 Jacob's shop sells stamps. _____
4 His mother is from Wales. _____
5 Mr Deng is Japanese. _____
6 He cooks and serves food. _____
7 Maria is Portuguese. _____
8 Anna is from Australia. _____

2 ▶ 1.5 Listen again. Complete the sentences with the numbers in the box. There are three numbers you don't need.

> 2 3 4 23 73
> 118 122 180 222

1 Jacob's shop sells _____ different types of sweets.
2 There are about _____ shops on Narborough Road.
3 People from _____ different countries have shops there.
4 Mr Deng has _____ restaurants.
5 Maria has _____ children.
6 Anna has _____ sisters.

READING

1 Read the blog on page 7 about an international home. Write the people's nationalities.

1 Suki _____
2 Lucja _____
3 Ryan _____
4 Simona _____
5 Marco _____

2 Circle the countries in the blog and underline the personal objects.

3 Are the sentences true (T), false (F) or doesn't say (DS)?

1 Suki is from France. _____
2 Five people live in Suki's flat. _____
3 Lucja speaks English well. _____
4 Suki is eighteen years old. _____
5 Ryan is a student. _____
6 Ryan works in a shop in Paris. _____
7 Simona doesn't like the weather in Brazil. _____
8 Simona's family live in Brazil. _____
9 Marco has a job in Paris. _____
10 Marco is Suki's boyfriend. _____

REVIEW and PRACTICE 1

HOME   **BLOG**   PODCASTS   ABOUT   CONTACT

Guest blogger Penny writes about people living in another country.

AN INTERNATIONAL HOME

All around the world, young people live and study away from their own homes. But what's it like living with people from other countries? I asked Suki, a photography student. Suki's from Vietnam, but she lives in France at the moment. Here's what she says about life in her international home.

I live in a flat in Paris with four other people. We're all from different countries, but we can all speak English really well. Our flat is very friendly and of course it has a great international atmosphere!

Lucja is from Poland and she's eighteen years old. She is a student, like me. She wants to be a dentist, but she really loves sweets! Lucja's a very happy person – I like her a lot. Here's a photo of her looking happy.

Ryan is twenty-five years old and he is from Ireland. He works in a café near our flat. He likes shopping and he loves shopping for clothes. Here's a photo of him wearing his favourite sunglasses. He thinks they are very cool!

Simona is from Brazil. She's twenty-one years old and she's a nurse. She doesn't like the weather here – she is always cold! I think she is unhappy because she can't see her family back home very often and she misses the sun. Here's Simona with her favourite umbrella – she takes it everywhere she goes!

Marco is from Italy. He's a student, too, but he wants to be a model. He's very handsome, isn't he? He's 23 years old and he likes cars, football and looking in the mirror!

Who do you live with? Tell us about them and where you live. Don't forget to send us some photographs, too!

UNIT 2

Work and play

2A LANGUAGE

GRAMMAR: Present simple: positive and negative

1 Choose the correct options to complete the sentences.

1 He _____ a taxi every evening.
   a drives   b drive
   c don't drive

2 My sister _____ English – she teaches Maths.
   a teach   b doesn't teach
   c teaches

3 I like my job, but it _____ very well.
   a doesn't pay   b pays
   c pay

4 At the weekend, I'm a tour guide. I _____ tourists around my city.
   a doesn't take   b takes
   c take

5 I speak French, but I _____ German.
   a don't speak   b speaks
   c speak

6 My mum _____ in a restaurant. She serves food.
   a work   b works
   c don't work

2 Complete the email with the correct present simple form of the verbs in brackets.

Hi Malin,

How are you? I am very busy at the moment. I ¹_____ (work) a lot of hours every day.

We ²_____ (have) a new teacher at school – Mrs Black. She ³_____ (teach) us English and French. She's very funny – everyone ⁴_____ (like) her. Mrs Black loves films, and we ⁵_____ (watch) a lot of interesting videos in her class. She ⁶_____ (live) here, though – she drives from London every day!

Mum and dad say 'hello'! They are busy, too. The restaurant is very popular and they ⁷_____ (serve) food and drink all day, every day!

Write soon,

Tamara

VOCABULARY: Jobs and job verbs

3 Order the letters to make words for jobs.

1 My mum's a TRODCO. She works in a hospital.
   _____

2 I'm a student, but on Friday nights I'm a GISREN with my band.
   _____

3 Ask a CAIMNECH to look at your car.
   _____

4 You must be good at Maths to work as an TONCANACUT.
   _____

5 I love travelling, so I want to be a THIGLF NETTANDTA.
   _____

6 I need to go to the STINTED. My teeth hurt.
   _____

7 My sister works as a TOESCIRENPIT in a hotel.
   _____

8 This light is broken. I must call an CAINCLEETRI.
   _____

4 Complete the sentences with job verbs.

1 Julio is a waiter. He _____ food in a restaurant.
2 My hairdresser _____ my hair every month.
3 Her aunt is a shop assistant. She _____ computers in a big shop.
4 He always _____ a suit to work because he's a lawyer.
5 Sonia is a tour guide. She _____ tourists with their questions.
6 His brother is a famous chef. He _____ food in the best hotel in Rome.

PRONUNCIATION: -s and -es endings

5 ▶ 2.1 Listen and circle the sound that you hear at the end of the underlined verb. Listen again, check and repeat.

1	Suki works in a restaurant.	/s/	/z/	/ɪz/
2	Anna watches TV every day.	/s/	/z/	/ɪz/
3	Sally helps her brother with his homework.	/s/	/z/	/ɪz/
4	Jean Paul drives an Italian car.	/s/	/z/	/ɪz/
5	Ester really likes chocolate.	/s/	/z/	/ɪz/
6	Roberto lives in Argentina.	/s/	/z/	/ɪz/
7	Max teaches Science.	/s/	/z/	/ɪz/
8	Turgay sells shoes.	/s/	/z/	/ɪz/

8

SKILLS 2B

LISTENING: Listening for names, places, days and times

1 ▶ 2.2 Listen to the conversation between two friends. Which names and places do you hear?

1 a Janine   b Jenny   c Joan
2 a Donna   b Donald   c Danny
3 a Mateo's   b Maria's   c Marco's
4 a Oxford   b Dartford   c Stratford
5 a Vicky   b Vinny   c Ricky

2 ▶ 2.2 Complete the sentences with *in*, *on* or *at*. Then listen again and check.

1 Vanessa plays tennis _____ seven o'clock.
2 She eats pizza _____ the Italian restaurant.
3 _____ Thursday night, she studies.
4 She is always _____ Oxford on Friday evenings.
5 Paul watches TV _____ Saturday evening.
6 Paul's favourite TV show starts _____ eight o'clock.

3 Match the words to make activities.

1 play   _____   a friends
2 read   _____   b to music
3 meet   _____   c the guitar
4 spend time _____   d English
5 go out   _____   e a film
6 see   _____   f with my family
7 study   _____   g for dinner
8 listen   _____   h the newspaper

4 Complete the sentences with six of the activities from exercise 3. Use the correct form of the verbs. Use positives and negatives.

1 She's the singer in the band and she also _____.
2 I _____ at home. I normally watch TV.
3 They _____ every day. They know a lot about the world.
4 She _____ at the new language academy in the city centre.
5 We _____ every week. We really like Italian restaurants.
6 Now that I am at university, I _____ except for the holidays.

5 ▶ 2.3 Read the sentences. <u>Underline</u> the words that only have the sound /ə/. Then listen and check.

1 Do you like music?
2 My sister's a teacher.
3 I want to play tennis!
4 What do you do in your free time?
5 He goes to school on Saturday morning.
6 Where is the cinema?

9

2C LANGUAGE

GRAMMAR: Present simple: questions

1 Complete the sentences with the words in the box.

> what   do   who   does (x 2)   how
> when   where   don't (x 2)

1 _____ you play football?
2 'Does she work here?' 'Yes, she _____.'
3 _____ do you go after work?
4 'Do they like dogs?' 'No, they _____.'
5 _____ does he live with?
6 _____ does the lesson start?
7 _____ your father speak Italian?
8 'Do you know Lisa?' 'No, we _____.'
9 _____ do they do at the weekend?
10 _____ do you say this word?

2 Order the words to make questions.

1 does / learn / where / he / Turkish
   _____?
2 Vietnam / you / come from / do
   _____?
3 she / a cat / does / have
   _____?
4 with / they / who / do / go out
   _____?
5 at / do / start work / eight / we
   _____?
6 you / do / why / to school / drive
   _____?
7 does / repair / where / she / cars
   _____?
8 suit / wear / he / a / does
   _____?

PRONUNCIATION: Auxiliary do/does in questions

3 Look at the pictures. Use the prompts to write questions about Carla.

1 where/live?
   _____
2 how/work?
   _____
3 when/home?
   _____
4 do/study/evening?
   _____
5 what/weekends?
   _____
6 who/cinema?
   _____

4 ▶ 2.4 Say the questions. How do we say *do* and *does*? Listen, check and repeat.

1 Do you like pizza?
2 Does he live with his parents?
3 What do you do at the weekend?
4 Do they speak Spanish?
5 Where does he work?
6 When do you watch TV?
7 Does your sister teach yoga?
8 Who do you spend time with in the evening?

SKILLS 2D

WRITING: Opening and closing an informal email

Hey Lucy,

How are things with you? Do you like your new home in London?

Here in Madrid everything is fine. I have a new flatmate. She is really nice and friendly, but I often think of you and wish you were here! Her name is Keira and she's from New Zealand. She's a good cook, but she doesn't make great chocolate cake like you!

I have a new part-time job. I'm a tour guide – I take people around Madrid and show them the sights. I work every afternoon, from 2 p.m. till 6 or 7 p.m. I really like my job, but I don't have a lot of free time at the moment! You can see me working in this photo.

In the evenings, I am quite tired, but I sometimes play tennis with Keira. At the weekends, I usually go to the cinema or go shopping.

Take care,

Maria

1 Read Maria's email then look at the phrases below. Are they opening (O) or closing (C) phrases?

1 Hi _____
2 Write soon with your news! _____
3 See you soon _____
4 Hello _____
5 Hi Marta _____
6 Love Freddie XXX _____

2 Find and <u>underline</u> the connectors in the email.

3 Choose the correct connectors.

1 I really like coffee *and* / *but* I don't like tea at all.
2 Is that your mother *and* / *or* is it your sister?
3 I go to school *and* / *so* I also have extra English lessons.
4 I'm from Spain, *but* / *and* I now live in Mexico.
5 I have two sisters: Vanessa *and* / *or* Sally.
6 Are you a teacher *or* / *but* a student?

4 Complete the email with *and*, *but* or *or*.

Hi Samantha,

I'm on holiday in Granada in Spain. Our holiday is really fun ¹_____ exciting ²_____ I wish you were here. I think it's the perfect place for you. You can choose to go to the beach ³_____ the mountains. The food ⁴_____ drink is lovely ⁵_____ people have lunch too late! They don't eat until 3 o'clock!!!

I will call you soon ⁶_____ write another email.

Bye,

Clare

5 Write an email to a friend in another country. Use *and*, *but* and *or* to connect your ideas. Include:

- an informal opening phrase
- information about your home, friends and free time
- an informal closing phrase.

11

2 REVIEW and PRACTICE

HOME   BLOG   PODCASTS   ABOUT   CONTACT

Tom and Sam talk about someone with an unusual job.

LISTENING

1 ▶ 2.5 Listen to the podcast about someone with an interesting job. Choose the correct answers.

1 Which sentence about Arabella is true?
   a She doesn't like going to the cinema.
   b Her hobby is also her job.
   c She reads a lot of newspapers.

2 What is Arabella's job?
   a She sells tickets at a cinema.
   b She's the manager of a magazine.
   c She writes about films.

3 What does Arabella say about Luke?
   a He really likes films.
   b He is her friend.
   c He doesn't talk a lot.

2 ▶ 2.5 Listen again. Complete the sentences with one or two words.

1 Arabella really loves her _____.
2 She writes about films for _____ and magazines.
3 She goes to the cinema _____ times a week.
4 She really likes horror _____.
5 After she sees a film, she likes to _____ it.
6 She also writes about _____.

3 ▶ 2.5 Order the words to make questions. Listen again and check your answers.

1 go / do / you / every night / to the cinema ?
   _____

2 what kind / like / you / do / of films ?
   _____

3 you / take / with you / a friend / do ?
   _____

4 have / you / do / another job ?
   _____

READING

1 Read the blog on page 13 about work and free time. Answer the questions.

1 What is Tom Fletcher's job?
2 Does Tom think we have a good work-life balance?
3 What does Tom think we need to spend more time doing?

2 Does Tom say the things below? Choose Yes or No.

1	Many people start work at seven o'clock.	Yes	No
2	People work more hours in winter.	Yes	No
3	Tom has his lunch at home.	Yes	No
4	Many people always feel tired.	Yes	No
5	Playing the guitar can make you feel good.	Yes	No
6	Meeting friends is a good idea.	Yes	No
7	We must all walk for fifteen minutes every day.	Yes	No
8	More free time is also good for your family.	Yes	No

3 Circle the free-time activities in the blog.

12

REVIEW and PRACTICE 2

HOME **BLOG** PODCASTS ABOUT CONTACT

Guest blogger Kate writes about ideas for a work–life balance.

Work or life?

Today, lots of people work or study for more than 50 hours a week. We don't have much free time in the week. But it's important to have a 'work–life balance' and to have some time away from work and studying. What can we do to make sure we don't work too much? Here are some ideas from life coach, Tom Fletcher.

People work really hard these days. Think about it – most of us read our work emails before breakfast! Then we work until seven o'clock. In winter, we probably don't see the sun! 60% of us take work home, too – and check our work emails late at night.

This is what a lot of people tell me about their day: 'I get up at six o'clock, eat lunch at my desk and go home at ten o'clock at night. I don't have time to go to a restaurant or to meet friends. I don't spend time with my family either – I'm always too busy. I want to relax, but there isn't enough time in the day. I'm always tired and I don't really enjoy my life at the moment.'

This isn't good for our minds or bodies. You need to make time for life, because it's important to do things that you enjoy. Listen to music, play the guitar, read a book or go to the cinema – these are things that make you feel good. And when you feel good, you can also work better.

Free-time activities don't need a lot of time – it's easy to make small changes to your day. Do you eat your lunch at your desk? Why not go out to a café – it's much more fun! Try to meet friends every day. Go for a fifteen-minute walk together. It makes you feel great and gives you more energy!

UNIT 3 People in my life

3A LANGUAGE

GRAMMAR: Adverbs and expressions of frequency

1 Order the words to make sentences.

1 always / is / your sister / late for school
   _____.

2 together / eats dinner / our family / once a week
   _____.

3 grandparents / sees / his / he / twice a month
   _____.

4 because / play tennis / I / never / I don't like it
   _____.

5 breakfast / they / eat / sometimes / a big
   _____.

6 in the kitchen / a day / helps my mother / my brother / three times
   _____.

2 Complete the conversation with adverbs and expressions of frequency.

Anas What do you ¹u_____ do in the summer holidays?

Sara I travel to the USA ²o_____ a year.

Anas Lucky you!

Sara Well, my family live there and I don't ³o_____ see them. But I visit my cousins ⁴t_____ a month because they live near me. What about you?

Anas I stay at home ⁵e_____ year.

Sara Really? Isn't that boring?

Anas Not at all! I work in a café three ⁶t_____ a week and I see my friends every day.

VOCABULARY: Family

3 Match the two parts of the sentences.

1 My aunt ____
2 My mother-in-law ____
3 My nephew ____
4 My grandparents ____
5 My niece ____
6 My sister-in-law ____

a is my husband's sister.
b is my brother's son.
c is my mother's sister.
d is my wife's mother.
e are my parents' mother and father.
f is my sister's daughter.

4 Complete the family words.

This is a photo of my family. This is me. I have one ¹s_____. Her name's Sal and this is her ²h_____, Ali. He's also my ³b_____-i_____-l_____, of course! They have two ⁴c_____ – both boys, called Casper and John – who are my ⁵n_____. My ⁶f_____ took the photo. His brother Fred is my favourite ⁷u_____!

PRONUNCIATION: Sentence stress

5 ▶ 3.1 Read the sentences. Stress the adverbs and expressions of frequency. Listen, check and repeat.

1 He sometimes visits his cousin.
2 We're never late.
3 I study English every day.
4 I see my nephew once a week.
5 We often eat Chinese food.
6 I usually go to the park with my niece.

SKILLS 3B

READING: Scanning a text

HOLIDAYS WITH A DIFFERENCE!

IT'S HOLIDAY TIME! READ ABOUT OUR ACTIVE HOLIDAYS
WHICH ONE DO YOU LIKE BEST?

A PONY TREKKING

Our pony trekking holidays are very popular. On these holidays, you stay in a quiet hotel in a beautiful place. Then you get up early and go pony trekking until 3 p.m. with one of our friendly guides. You also learn all about pony care.

C TAKE A BREAK – WITH A YOGA HOLIDAY

Are you busy at work? Are you always tired? Relax and spend time with other people who love yoga. You stay in a beautiful small house beside the sea. In the morning you practise yoga and go swimming in the sea. In the afternoon and evening you eat our healthy food (it's also delicious!).

B SINGING IN SUMMER!

Do you love music? Then this holiday is for you. On this special holiday you sing in a group every morning for two hours. Then, in the afternoon, you give group concerts in the town centre. In the evening, you relax and sometimes go dancing, too. It's a lot of fun!

D ARTS AND CRAFTS

Our arts and crafts holiday is for people who love to make things. Every morning you learn a different craft and in the afternoon you go on trips to visit different artists. In the evening you show the other students your work. It's a fun holiday and it's interesting, too!

1 Scan the text. On which holiday do you:
1 eat delicious food? _____
2 dance in the evenings? _____
3 stay in a hotel? _____
4 learn different crafts? _____

2 Are the sentences true (T), false (F) or doesn't say (DS)?
1 On the pony trekking holiday, you go riding with a guide. _____
2 You can go swimming in the evening on the pony trekking holiday. _____
3 You meet people from different countries on the singing holiday. _____
4 On the singing holiday, you can relax in the evenings. _____
5 You buy and cook your own food on the yoga holiday. _____
6 On the yoga holiday, you stay near the sea. _____
7 On the arts and crafts holiday, other people can look at your work. _____
8 You make different things in the afternoon on the arts and crafts holiday. _____

3 Complete the sentences with *also* or *too*.
1 These holidays sound good! I like the yoga holiday and the singing holiday, _____.
2 I want to go on the pony trekking holiday and I _____ want to go on the yoga holiday.
3 I like ponies and I _____ like quiet hotels.
4 On the arts and crafts holiday, you make art and you look at other people's work, _____.
5 Singing is fun and it's relaxing, _____.
6 Yoga is interesting and it's _____ very good for you.

15

3C LANGUAGE

GRAMMAR: *love, like, hate, enjoy, don't mind* + noun/*-ing* form

1 Complete the text with the *-ing* form of the verbs in brackets.

I love ¹_____ (live) with my family! We're all very happy. My dad enjoys ²_____ (drive) his taxi for work every day. My mum's very busy so I don't mind ³_____ (make) breakfast for my little sister and ⁴_____ (take) her to the park sometimes. My brother, Pat, loves ⁵_____ (run) in the park and he really likes ⁶_____ (swim) in the outside pool there – but he hates ⁷_____ (go) to school! At weekends we all enjoy ⁸_____ (be) together. Sometimes I like to be alone though. I love ⁹_____ (sit) with a book or ¹⁰_____ (plan) my future!

2 Complete the sentences with *love / not like / hate / enjoy / don't mind* + *-ing* form of the verbs in the box.

study   help   meet   work   spend
play   visit   relax   watch   eat

1 Do you _____ time with your family at the weekend? ☺

2 I _____ vegetables, but I like chips more! ☺

3 My sister _____ Maths and never does her homework. ☹ ☹

4 Do you _____ in the evening after work? ☺

5 We _____ our friends for coffee in the new café in town. ☺ ☺

6 Jaime _____ the dentist so he doesn't go very often. ☹ ☹

7 His uncle makes cars. He _____ in a factory. ☹

8 They _____ their mum with the shopping and cooking. ☺

9 I _____ films at home, but I go to the cinema every week. ☹

10 Does your brother _____ online games? ☺ ☺

VOCABULARY: Activities (2)

3 Order the letters to make words for activities.

1 OG PSHOPNIG
_____

2 SITIV A LLAGYRE
_____

3 LYAP HET LINVIO
_____

4 OG GLIBWON
_____

5 OD GOYA
_____

6 HEAV A CINCIP
_____

7 APLY LOVELYBLLA
_____

8 ISITV STERILAVE
_____

4 Complete the sentences with the correct verbs.

1 What great weather! Do you want to _____ a barbecue?

2 When it rains on holiday, I like to _____ a museum.

3 I never _____ golf – I think it's a boring game.

4 My girlfriend loves to _____ swimming, but I hate the water!

5 I don't have time to cook, so I often _____ a takeaway for dinner.

6 I want to _____ dancing tonight. There's a great DJ playing!

7 Do you want to _____ cycling at the weekend?

8 His niece wants to learn to _____ karate next year.

PRONUNCIATION: *-ing* forms

5 ▶ 3.2 Say the sentences. How do we say the *-ing* forms? Listen, check and repeat.

1 I don't mind playing tennis.

2 We love visiting our grandmother.

3 I don't like being late.

4 I love reading stories.

5 I like running.

6 I hate watching TV.

7 I don't mind going to school.

8 I enjoy doing sport.

SKILLS 3D

SPEAKING: Accepting or declining an invitation

1 Look at the clocks and write the times.

1 It's _____
2 It's _____
3 It's _____
4 It's _____
5 _____
6 _____
7 _____
8 _____

2 ▶ 3.3 Listen to the conversation between two friends. Are the sentences true or false?

1	Pablo suggests going for a walk.	True	False
2	Sara accepts Pablo's invitation for tonight.	True	False
3	Sara must visit her grandfather.	True	False
4	Pablo suggests tomorrow morning.	True	False
5	They agree to meet at one o'clock.	True	False

3 ▶ 3.3 Complete the lines from the conversation with the words in the box. Then listen again and check.

| how | let's | can't | time |
| say | about | plans | want |

1 Do you have _____ after work today?
2 Do you _____ to go to the cinema with me?
3 Tonight? Oh, I'm sorry, I _____.
4 What _____ tomorrow?
5 _____ about having lunch with me?
6 Great, _____ go together.
7 What _____ is good for you?
8 Let's _____ one o'clock.

4 Match 1–5 with a–e to make conversations.

1 Do you want to come to my birthday party on Saturday? _____
2 Would you like to come to the match with me? I've got two tickets. _____
3 How about going to the new burger restaurant together? _____
4 Do you want to have coffee together later? _____
5 Are you free for lunch today? _____

a I'd love to, but I don't eat meat. Sorry!
b Cool! I love football.
c Sure!
d Yes, I'd love to!
e Saturday? I'm sorry, I can't.

5 ▶ 3.4 Listen and check. Then say if the people accept (A) or decline (D) the invitations in each conversation.

1 _____
2 _____
3 _____
4 _____
5 _____

6 ▶ 3.4 Listen again and repeat the conversations in exercise 4. Copy the intonation to sound enthusiastic or sorry.

17

3 REVIEW and PRACTICE

LISTENING

1 ▶ 3.5 Listen to the podcast about a family business called 'Swish'. Number a–h in the order you hear them (1–8).

a brother ____
b sisters ____
c mother ____
d grandmother ____
e grandfather ____
f cousins ____
g sister-in-law ____
h aunts ____

2 ▶ 3.5 Listen again and choose the correct answers.

1 Why do people enjoy going to Swish?
  a The haircuts are very cheap.
  b The hairdressers are friendly.
  c There's a nice atmosphere.
2 How many family members does Mila think work in the hairdresser?
  a ten
  b eleven
  c twelve
3 How many aunts does Mila have?
  a two
  b three
  c four
4 What does Mila do at Swish?
  a She cuts hair.
  b She makes coffee.
  c She does lots of different things.
5 Does the family enjoy working together?
  a sometimes
  b usually
  c always
6 Why are there sometimes problems?
  a because of money
  b because of customers
  c because they are busy

READING

1 Read the blog on page 19 about spending time with your family. Write R (Roberto), M (Mariella) or B (both). Who:

1 doesn't like playing golf? ____
2 is busy at work? ____
3 likes going out with friends? ____
4 doesn't enjoy going dancing? ____
5 doesn't like shopping? ____
6 goes cycling three times a month? ____

2 Are the sentences true (T) or false (F)?

1 Roberto doesn't like music. ____
2 Mariella and Roberto hardly ever talk together. ____
3 Mariella plays golf with her friends. ____
4 Roberto likes playing golf with his daughter. ____
5 Roberto has a lot of free time. ____
6 Mariella and Roberto sometimes cycle to the beach. ____
7 Mariella talks to her father about school. ____
8 Roberto enjoys going cycling with Mariella. ____

3 Circle the adverbs and expressions of frequency in the blog.

REVIEW and PRACTICE 3

HOME BLOG PODCASTS ABOUT CONTACT

Guest blogger Simon writes about how a father and a daughter spend time together.

Family time

In today's busy world, it isn't always easy for families to spend time together. So why not try doing your mother's, father's, son's or daughter's hobby with them? Read about how Mariella and her dad, Roberto, enjoy some free time together.

Mariella

My dad plays golf three times a week. He's always at the golf course. I don't know why! I don't think it's a great sport – you don't run, there's no music and I don't like the clothes people wear!

I don't see my dad very often and sometimes I don't know what to talk about with him. That's why I like coming here together, because there's always something to talk about – where the golf ball is going, for example! When we're at home, I'm usually on my phone talking to friends. But I never look at my phone when we play golf!

I play golf with dad about once a week. I don't really like it very much, but I like being with him and I know he enjoys it, too.

Roberto

I have a very busy job and I hardly ever have free time. But Mariella doesn't often talk to me. She has a lot of friends and she enjoys going out with them. And she never stops talking on her phone! She loves going dancing, too – but it's not my favourite thing! It's probably a bit boring to go out with your father. So it's great that Mariella plays golf with me. It's very special.

Mariella loves cycling, so we also go cycling together three times a month. Mariella always decides where to go. Sometimes we take our bikes to the beach, sometimes to the hills. We often talk – usually about things like school or work. Sometimes we talk about our favourite music. I'm happy to do Mariella's hobby with her. But I hope she never asks me to go shopping with her. I hate going shopping!

UNIT 4 Home and away

4A LANGUAGE

GRAMMAR: Prepositions of time

1 Complete the sentences with the words in the box.

| in (x2)   on (x2)   to   at (x2)   from |

1 _____ Friday nights, I usually have a takeaway.
2 The bank is open _____ 10 a.m. to 4 p.m.
3 School is always closed _____ August.
4 _____ the winter, I don't go out very often.
5 We study a lot _____ the weekend.
6 I'm always tired _____ Monday morning.
7 Where were you _____ midnight last night?
8 The outdoor swimming pool is open from May _____ October.

2 Complete the text with prepositions of time.

A typical day? Well, I usually get up ¹_____ 7 a.m., but ²_____ summer it's lighter, so I get up earlier – maybe 6.30 a.m. I have a job in a café – I serve food to customers.
I work ³_____ 10 a.m. ⁴_____ 6 p.m. every day in the week – ⁵_____ Monday ⁶_____ Friday. After work, ⁷_____ 6 p.m., I usually meet my friends. ⁸_____ Friday nights we go to a restaurant or to the cinema. ⁹_____ July, the café is closed for one month, so I don't work at all. It's also closed ¹⁰_____ Christmas. Then, my typical day is very different!

VOCABULARY: Daily routine verbs

3 Order the verbs 1–8 to make a typical day.

a get home _____
b leave work _____
c have dinner _____
d go to bed _____
e have breakfast _____
f go to work _____
g go to sleep _____
h get up _____

4 Order the letters to make daily routine verbs.

1 I **egt deserds** after a big breakfast.
2 Do you watch TV before you **og ot loshoc**?
3 My brother doesn't often **veah clunh** because he's busy.
4 Yolanda likes to **kwae pu** early and read a magazine.
5 On Sunday, before I **teg pu**, I have a cup of coffee.
6 Does he **vahe a roshew** every morning?
7 Our mum sometimes **sha a hatb** before bed.
8 When they **evale closho** they play in the park.

PRONUNCIATION: Sentence stress

5 ▶ 4.1 Read the sentences. Which words are stressed? Listen, check and repeat.

1 I get up at eleven o'clock.
2 I go to school from nine o'clock to three o'clock.
3 We have breakfast at 7.30.
4 He cycles to work in the summer.
5 I play football on Saturday afternoons.
6 She wakes up at eight.

20

SKILLS 4B

LISTENING: Listening for the main idea

1 ▶ 4.2 Listen to a conversation about Hong Kong. Tick (✓) the different types of weather you hear.

a ____

b ____

c ____

d ____

e ____

f ____

2 ▶ 4.2 Listen again. Are the sentences true (T) or false (F)?

1 The weather is always the same in Hong Kong. ____
2 Fiona doesn't like hot weather. ____
3 Fiona is a student. ____
4 It never rains in Hong Kong. ____
5 Typhoons bring bad weather. ____

3 Complete the weather words for a–f in exercise 1.

a s_____g
b s_____y
c r_____g
d f_____y
e w_____y
f c_____y

4 Order the letters to make seasons. Which words from exercise 3 describe the weather in your country in each season?

1 RETWIN _____
2 GRINPS _____
3 UNMATU _____
4 REMUMS _____

5 ▶ 4.3 Read the sentences. <u>Underline</u> the words which you think will be stressed. Listen and check.

1 What's the climate like there?
2 There are four seasons.
3 The weather is too hot for me.
4 It always rains here!
5 Is Hong Kong a beautiful city?

21

4C LANGUAGE

GRAMMAR: Present continuous

1 Choose the correct options to complete the sentences.

1 I _____ a great time in New York.
   a has   b having   c 'm having

2 'Where's Peter?' 'He _____ his mother at the moment.'
   a 's helping   b helps   c are helping

3 'Are we eating lunch here?' 'No, we _____.'
   a don't   b aren't   c isn't

4 Where _____ you going right now?
   a is   b are   c do

5 I'm _____ enjoying this film.
   a doesn't   b not   c no

6 Are you _____ to the party on Friday?
   a come   b comes   c coming

7 Laila's _____ tonight, so she isn't here.
   a work   b works   c working

8 _____ they having a karate lesson today?
   a Do   b Are   c Is

9 'Is he listening to the radio?' 'No, he _____.'
   a is   b doesn't   c isn't

10 They _____ going clubbing in town this week.
   a aren't   b not   c don't

2 Order the words to make statements and questions.

1 in / we / the classroom / sitting / are / now
   _____.

2 their holiday / India / aren't / they / spending / in
   _____.

3 today / are / enjoying / the children / school
   _____?

4 she / the moment / listening / at / isn't
   _____.

5 visiting / you / this week / are / new places
   _____?

6 right / is / now / snowing / it
   _____?

7 walking / today / not / the dog / I'm
   _____.

8 camping / he / is / this year / going
   _____.

PRONUNCIATION: Linking consonants and vowels

3 ▶ 4.4 Underline the words that are linked. Listen, check and repeat.

1 What are you doing tomorrow?
2 I'm going away next weekend.
3 She's eating her breakfast.
4 It isn't very warm today.
5 I'm getting up late tomorrow.
6 He's asking his teacher.

4 Write sentences to describe what the people (1–8) in the picture are doing.

22

SKILLS | 4D

WRITING: Describing a photo

Hey Rob,

How are you? I'm having a great time in London. I'm doing summer school – I love learning English! The weather isn't very hot and it rains a lot, but [1]_____'s good weather for learning and sightseeing.

I'm really busy – there's so much to do! Lessons start at 9 a.m. and [2]_____ finish at 1 p.m. I usually get up early and go for a walk before breakfast. I learn English with the other students all morning, then [3]_____ stop for lunch. After lunch, we all go into the centre of London to see the sights. In the evening we have dinner together. Then we go to the park or play football.

I'm sending you a few photos. In this photo, I'm playing football with my new friend, George. George is from Serbia – [4]_____'s really good at sport. This is a photo of my classroom with my English teacher, Joanna. [5]_____'s really funny and I enjoy her lessons. Here's a photo of my classmates in the park – [6]_____'s a beautiful place to relax.

Are you in London at the moment? Can we meet some afternoon?

See you soon,

Fernando

1 Read Fernando's email. Complete 1–6 with the correct pronouns.

2 Number a–e in the order Fernando does the things (1–5).

a describes his daily routine _____

b asks Rob to meet him _____

c talks about the weather _____

d describes some photographs _____

e asks Rob a friendly question _____

3 Complete the sentences with the correct words.

1 In _____ photo, we're playing in the park.

2 This photo is _____ my friend George.

3 _____ is a photo of my teacher, Joanna.

4 _____ this photo, we're having lunch.

5 Here's _____ photo of London.

6 This photo _____ of the other students in my class.

4 You are at a sports camp. Write an email to a friend. Use personal pronouns to avoid repeating words and names.

Talk about:
- the weather
- your daily routine
- some photos and what you are doing in them.

23

4 REVIEW and PRACTICE

HOME BLOG **PODCASTS** ABOUT CONTACT

Tom and Sam talk about sleep.

LISTENING

1 ▶ 4.5 Listen to the podcast about sleep. Tick (✓) the things Dr Patel talks about.

a using a computer ___
b lunch ___
c doing yoga ___
d teenagers ___
e having a bath ___
f having a shower ___
g watching TV ___
h breakfast ___

2 ▶ 4.5 Listen again. Does Dr Patel say the things below? Choose Yes or No.

1	Most teenagers don't get enough sleep.	Yes	No
2	Most teenagers need eight hours sleep a night.	Yes	No
3	Dr Patel eats a big lunch.	Yes	No
4	Dr Patel has dinner late at night.	Yes	No
5	He has a bath every evening.	Yes	No
6	He goes to bed after eleven o'clock.	Yes	No
7	He only works on his computer until six o'clock.	Yes	No
8	The light from your phone can stop you relaxing.	Yes	No

READING

1 Read the blog on page 25 about the weather in two different countries. Match headings 1–5 with paragraphs A–E.

1 Different weather, different clothes ___
2 Making new friends in a new country ___
3 Sport at home and away ___
4 Different lives in two countries ___
5 Summer and winter weather ___

2 Tick (✓) the true sentences.

1 Patrice is a student from Canada. ___
2 He's spending Christmas in Australia. ___
3 He thinks life in Australia is similar to life in Canada. ___
4 He's wearing warm clothes at the beach today. ___
5 He hates the winter in Canada. ___
6 The weather in Canada is very different in summer and winter. ___
7 Patrice doesn't have many friends in Australia. ___
8 He never goes surfing in Canada. ___

3 Circle the weather and the seasons vocabulary in the blog.

24

REVIEW and PRACTICE 4

HOME   BLOG   PODCASTS   ABOUT   CONTACT

Guest blogger Marc writes about the weather in different countries.

NORTH AND SOUTH

What's the weather like in your country? Do you think the weather changes how you feel? What happens when people move from a hot country to a cold country, or from a cold place to somewhere really hot? Twenty-year-old Patrice Chiffre told me about moving from Canada to Australia.

A I come from Calgary, a city in Canada, but now I'm studying at university in Australia. The weather in these countries isn't the same at all! And I think it changes how people live and work in these places.

C Where I'm living in Australia at the moment, there is a wet season and a dry season. The wet season is really hot, and the dry season is a little colder. But at home in Canada, the winters are long, dark and really cold. The short and sunny summers bring a big change, so people often eat more healthily, do more exercise and get up early in the morning. I love the summers in Canada – they are full of energy, festivals and parties!

D People spend a lot of time outside in Australia, so it's easy to meet people and make new friends. Of course it's different in Canada, especially in winter. People stay inside more, and don't see their friends very often. I'm meeting lots of new people here in Australia!

B First, the months and seasons aren't the same. In December in Canada, people wear warm coats and hats and some people have Christmas dinner next to a big fire. But in Australia, January is summer and July is winter. Today is the beginning of February and everyone is wearing T-shirts and shorts. I'm eating lunch by the sea with my friends and we're enjoying the sunny weather! People often spend Christmas at the beach here.

E One thing I love about Canada is all the snow and ice we have in winter. I love going skiing, too. It hardly ever snows here in Australia, but I enjoy going surfing – that's something I can't do at home!

25

UNIT 5
What are you wearing?

5A — LANGUAGE

GRAMMAR: Present simple and present continuous

1 Choose the correct options to complete the sentences.

1 Ramona is Spanish. She *is coming from / comes from* Spain.

2 My aunt *doesn't work / isn't working* near her home.

3 *I eat / I'm eating* a big breakfast every morning.

4 'Where is Katia?' 'There she is. *She's wearing / She wears* a blue jacket.'

5 Hello! *Are you looking / Do you look* for me?

6 We *don't visit / aren't visiting* our grandparents very often.

7 *Is he watching / Does he watch* TV at the moment?

8 They *aren't selling / don't sell* magazines in this shop.

2 Complete the conversation with the present simple or present continuous form of the verbs in brackets.

Andy Hi! I'm Andy. ¹ _____ (you/have) a good time?

Mara Yes, it's a great party! My name's Mara.

Andy Hi Mara! Where ² _____ (you/come from)?

Mara I'm from Brazil, but I ³ _____ (study) in London this summer. What about you?

Andy I'm Welsh, but I ⁴ _____ (not live) in Wales. I ⁵ _____ (work) here with my parents for a few months.

Mara That's interesting! What ⁶ _____ (they/do)?

Andy They ⁷ _____ (repair) cars. We ⁸ _____ (not make) a lot of money, but my mum ⁹ _____ (enjoy) working with the family!

Mara That's brilliant! My mum ¹⁰ _____ (not have) a job at the moment, but she wants to be a singer!

VOCABULARY: Clothes and ordinal numbers

3 Match definitions 1–8 with clothes a–h.

1 You might wear these on your legs at the beach. _____

2 This makes your neck warm on a cold day. _____

3 You can put these on your hands when it's cold. _____

4 Men often wear this at work. _____

5 You need these on your feet in the snow. _____

6 You can wear this on your head in summer or winter. _____

7 You wear this around the top of your trousers. _____

8 When it's hot and sunny, people wear these on their feet. _____

a sandals

b belt

c hat

d gloves

e scarf

f shorts

g tie

h boots

4 Write the words next to the ordinal numbers.

1 11th _____

2 3rd _____

3 12th _____

4 29th _____

5 40th _____

6 36th _____

7 28th _____

8 19th _____

9 31st _____

10 14th _____

PRONUNCIATION: Dates

5 ▶5.1 Underline the stressed words. Listen, check and repeat.

1 It's May the fifteenth.

2 It's December the sixth.

3 It's the thirtieth of November.

4 It's the eleventh of April.

5 It's October the twelfth.

6 It's the twenty-third of June.

7 It's the sixteenth of February.

8 It's July the twenty-ninth.

9 It's the fourteenth of January.

10 It's August the thirty-first.

SKILLS 5B

READING: Identifying facts and opinions

ALL ABOUT CLOTHES ...

I'm Marta and I'm a fashion blogger from Chile. I love making my own clothes and posting pictures of them on this blog!

A I write my blog at home. I need to wear warm clothes because my house is cold. In this picture, I'm wearing my favourite working clothes – I call this my uniform! I think this dress is ¹*tianlrilb* – it's really long and it keeps me warm, too. My best friend makes jewellery – in this picture I'm wearing one of her necklaces.

B I love walking and there are lots of mountains in Chile. I often go hiking at the weekend. Here I am in my favourite hat and walking trousers. I think they're ²*tearg!*

C I'm not just a fashion blogger! I also have a part-time job. I work as a waitress in a café near my home. I can wear what I like because there isn't a uniform. I usually wear this black skirt and smart white top because I think it looks ³*lvoyel*. Do you like my shoes?

D This is my ⁴*eautfilub* little brother! He's only five years old. I really like making clothes for him. He's wearing green trousers and a T-shirt because these are his favourite clothes.

E The clothes I make aren't always good. This dress is horrible – it's ⁵*sranibregams!* It's too big for me and it's also too short. It's ⁶*fulwa*, I know, but everyone makes mistakes!

1

2

3

4

5

1 Read Marta's blog. Match paragraphs A–E with pictures 1–5.

A _____
B _____
C _____
D _____
E _____

2 Order the letters in 1–6 in the blog to make adjectives.

1 _____
2 _____
3 _____
4 _____
5 _____
6 _____

3 Read the sentences from some of Marta's other blog posts. Are they opinion (O) or fact (F)?

1 I agree that shopping for clothes is boring. _____
2 There are 25 clothes shops in my town. _____
3 I think that my big brother's clothes are terrible! _____
4 My birthday is on 23rd June. I want to get some new shoes! _____
5 I don't think that British people have very good clothes. _____
6 My mother has a job as a nurse. _____

27

5C LANGUAGE

GRAMMAR: *can* and *can't*

1 Complete the sentences with *can* or *can't*.

1 I _____ see it because I'm not wearing my glasses.

2 '_____ you help me, please?' 'Yes, of course!'

3 'Where is the nearest café?' 'I'm sorry, we're not from here. We _____ tell you.'

4 Anita is a great photographer. She _____ take really good photos.

5 'Can Miguel cook Chinese food?' 'No, he _____.'

6 '_____ they speak French?' 'Yes, a little.'

7 Are you hungry? You _____ have some of my pizza if you like.

8 You _____ buy this book, but you can download it.

9 'Can you see the sea from your house?' 'Yes, we _____.'

10 She can go to the club tonight, but she _____ stay too late.

2 Complete the sentences with *can* or *can't* and the verbs in the box.

> run   read   teach   come   play   go out
> hear   understand   ask   borrow

1 '_____ I _____ you a question?' 'Yes, what is it?'

2 Sarah _____ _____ football, but she likes watching it.

3 I'm going to Italy next week. _____ you _____ me some Italian words?

4 'Can you _____ this letter?' 'No, I _____. The writing is really small.'

5 I _____ _____ very fast because I'm wearing sandals!

6 Alina has a lot of homework, so she _____ _____ tonight.

7 _____ I _____ your book? It looks really interesting.

8 They _____ _____ to my party on Saturday – they're on holiday.

9 'Can you _____ that noise?' 'Yes, I _____ – what is it?'

10 I _____ _____ you – you're speaking too fast.

VOCABULARY: Hobbies

3 Match the two parts of the sentences.

1 My friend Anita makes   _____
2 Our grandmother collects   _____
3 His English teacher plays   _____
4 Her sister takes   _____
5 What does he draw   _____
6 Can you bake   _____

a pictures of?

b really good photos of animals.

c a cake for my birthday?

d jewellery like bracelets and necklaces.

e coins. She has over a thousand!

f the drums in a band.

4 Complete the sentences with the correct verbs.

1 At school, we _____ blogs about what we are learning.

2 Daniel _____ pictures of his girlfriend in beautiful colours.

3 My sister _____ online games for hours.

4 Can you _____ chess? Do you want to learn?

5 Costa's aunt wants to _____ him a jumper for the winter.

6 Not many people _____ stamps these days.

PRONUNCIATION: *can* and *can't*

5 ▶ 5.2 Say the sentences. How do we say *can* and *can't*? Listen, check and repeat.

1 I can't sew clothes. Can you?

2 'Can you speak Chinese?' 'Yes, I can.'

3 John can't sing, but he can play the drums.

4 My mum can cook really well.

5 I can dance, but I can't sing.

6 My dad can leave work early this week.

7 'Can your brother play the violin?' 'No, he can't.'

8 You can't buy a new top today.

SKILLS 5D

SPEAKING: Offering help

1 ▶5.3 Listen to Tim talking about shopping for his holiday. Tick (✓) the clothes you hear.

a coat ___
b boots ___
c scarf ___
d shirt ___
e gloves ___
f jumper ___
g sandals ___
h shorts ___
i socks ___
j T-shirt ___

2 Complete the questions with the words in the box. Then match them with answers a–f below.

sell in colours pay changing much

1 Do you have it _____ blue? ___
2 Do you _____ scarves? ___
3 What _____ are there? ___
4 How _____ is this green one? ___
5 Where are the men's _____ rooms, please? ___
6 Can I _____ with this credit card? ___

   a They're all 30 euros.
   b I'll show you.
   c We do, yes.
   d Just a moment, I'll check. Yes, here you are.
   e Certainly, sir.
   f We have these in black, red and green.

3 ▶5.3 Listen and check.

4 ▶5.4 Listen to 5 conversations. What does the shop assistant do? Choose the correct option.

	asks if the customer needs help	says that he/she will do something
1		
2		
3		
4		
5		

5 ▶5.4 Read the conversations. What do you think the shop assistant says? Then listen again and check.

1
Shop assistant Are you alright? Do you _____ any help?
Customer Yes – do you sell coats?
2
Shop assistant Can I help _____?
Customer Yes, please. How much are these pyjamas?
3
Customer Can I pay with this credit card?
Shop assistant Just a moment, I'll _____.
4
Customer Where are the men's changing rooms?
Shop assistant I'll _____ you where they are.
5
Customer Do you have this suit in medium?
Shop assistant _____ me ask my colleague.

6 ▶5.4 Listen again. Repeat what the shop assistant says.

5 REVIEW and PRACTICE

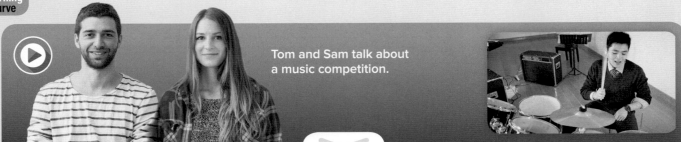

HOME   BLOG   PODCASTS   ABOUT   CONTACT

Tom and Sam talk about a music competition.

LISTENING

1 🔊 5.5 Listen to the podcast about a music competition. Choose the correct answers.

1 How old is Tony Pia?
   a 17
   b 18
   c 20
2 What instrument can Tony play well?
   a the drums
   b the piano
   c the guitar
3 When is the final of the music competition?
   a 30 June
   b 30 January
   c 13 June

2 🔊 5.5 Listen again. Complete the sentences with one or two words.

1 The competition is called Young Drummer of _____.
2 Young people from all over _____ enter the competition.
3 Tony is feeling a bit _____.
4 Tony's mum can play the _____.
5 Tony plays the drums every _____.
6 Playing the drums makes Tony feel _____ and full of energy.

READING

1 Read the blog on page 31 about what to wear for a job interview. Answer the questions.

1 What is Angela Santo's job?
2 What is Norbert Szil's job?
3 Which person's clothes does Angela prefer?
4 Which person's clothes does Norbert prefer?

2 Are the sentences correct? Choose Yes or No.

1	Angela and Norbert like Jo's hat.	Yes	No
2	Angela doesn't like Jo's scarf.	Yes	No
3	Norbert likes Jo's scarf and top.	Yes	No
4	Norbert thinks Dan looks good.	Yes	No
5	Angela thinks Dan is wearing great clothes for an interview.	Yes	No
6	Angela likes all Isa's clothes.	Yes	No
7	Angela thinks skirts are better than trousers for an interview.	Yes	No
8	Norbert thinks Isa's clothes are good for a job in fashion.	Yes	No

3 Circle the clothes vocabulary in the blog.

REVIEW and PRACTICE 5

HOME BLOG PODCASTS ABOUT CONTACT

Guest blogger Ethan hears about wearing the right clothes.

Dress for success

You have an interview for the job of your dreams. Congratulations! So, what are you thinking of wearing on the big day? It can be easy to make bad choices. Angela Santo is a hotel manager and Norbert Szil has a fashion business. They tell me how to dress for success.

Jo

Angela I'm not at all sure about this one. Why is she wearing a hat?' I don't think that hats are a great idea – not for a job interview. And I don't think the scarf is very tidy. It looks a little informal, too.

Norbert I agree with Angela about the hat. I don't agree with her about the rest of the clothes, though. This woman is wearing very smart clothes and I think the scarf and top are good together. She looks cool!

Dan

Norbert This man is carrying an old case. It's not at all smart! It looks awful! I think he's wearing a suit, shirt and tie, but are those trainers on his feet? This is never a good look, but for a job interview it's terrible!

Angela I agree with Norbert. This man does not look smart. Are you sure he's going to a job interview?

Isa

Angela This woman has got it right! The skirt is great – not too long or short – and it's dark blue, which is a great colour for interviews. She's wearing a nice jacket, too. Suits are great for interviews, and women can wear trouser suits or skirt suits.

Norbert Is this woman looking for a job in a bank? I think she'll do well. There's just one thing – I can't imagine her working in fashion. Her clothes are a bit boring. Some colour is always a great thing, and how about some jewellery?

UNIT 6 Homes and cities

6A LANGUAGE

GRAMMAR: *there is/there are, some/any* and prepositions of place

1 Complete the text with the words in the box.

| there are | are | are there | there's |
| is | any | there | some |

So, this is my bedroom – I really like it! ¹_____ a window by my bed, so I can see outside. Opposite the bed is a TV. I love watching TV in bed at night! ²_____ some cupboards, too, for my clothes. ³_____ any shelves? Yes, there ⁴_____ – look! There are ⁵_____ shelves beside the bed. There aren't ⁶_____ books on them because I don't like reading. ⁷_____ are lots of DVDs though. And ⁸_____ there a desk? No, I do my homework downstairs on the big table!

2 Choose the preposition which is **not** correct.

1 The boy is *in front of / behind / between* the door.
2 The table is *next to / opposite / in* a small window.
3 The big chair is *on / behind / in front of* the cupboard.
4 Is his book *under / between / next to* your shopping bag?
5 My house is *between / under / opposite* the park and the station.
6 Two apples are *in / under / on* the table.
7 Your cat is *behind / on / between* the sofa.
8 Is your flat *next to / between / on* those two shops?
9 Our teacher is *in / next to / in front of* the big desk.
10 Her phone is *behind / in / under* the TV.

VOCABULARY: Rooms and furniture

3 Order the letters to make words for rooms or furniture.

1 Is there a DROBRAWE in your bedroom?
_____
2 There are a lot of old books and toys in the TENSMEAB of our house.
_____
3 When it's sunny I like sitting outside on the YLBCAON.
_____
4 We've got a AGGARE where my parents keep their car.
_____
5 Julia's in the THRABOMO. She's having a shower.
_____
6 Their house has a LITTOE upstairs and one downstairs.
_____

4 Write the words for the definitions.

1 You look at your face in this.
 m_____
2 You can wash your clothes in this.
 w_____ m_____
3 This is a room at the top of a house.
 a_____
4 You walk up and down these.
 s_____
5 You eat food here.
 d_____ r_____
6 There are often flowers and trees here.
 g_____
7 You can do your homework here.
 s_____
8 You cook food here.
 k_____

PRONUNCIATION: *there's/there are*

5 ▶ 6.1 Say the sentences. How do we say *there's* and *there are*? Listen again and repeat.

1 There's a bed in the living room.
2 There are some chairs next to the table.
3 Is there a sofa in your bedroom?
4 Are there any shelves? No, there aren't.
5 There are five tables in their house.
6 Is there any food in the cupboard?
7 There's a cooker in his room.
8 There isn't a hall in his apartment.

SKILLS 6B

LISTENING: Identifying key points

1 ▶ 6.2 Listen to a TV show about houses. Tick (✓) the key points the speakers talk about.

a the furniture ____
b the colours of the rooms ____
c spending time with the family ____
d the garden ____
e the size of the house ____

2 ▶ 6.2 Listen again. Complete the sentences.

1 The windows are really big and _____.
2 At first, the house had two _____.
3 Loretta has _____ children.
4 The presenter thinks their furniture is really _____.
5 Loretta's husband really likes _____ furniture.
6 Loretta painted the bathroom and _____.
7 The furniture was _____ expensive.
8 Loretta loves sitting on the _____ in the summer.

3 Read the sentences. Write the full form or contracted form of the underlined words.

1 He's very busy at work. _____
2 There is a picture on the wall. _____
3 The table is near the window. _____
4 It's a sunny day today. _____
5 I do not like vegetables. _____
6 I'm nineteen years old. _____
7 She is not very friendly. _____
8 They're not cheap at all. _____

4 Put the adjectives in the box into seven pairs of opposite meanings.

| clean light narrow uncomfortable dirty cheap modern quiet heavy expensive traditional wide noisy comfortable |

1 _____ _____
2 _____ _____
3 _____ _____
4 _____ _____
5 _____ _____
6 _____ _____
7 _____ _____

33

6C LANGUAGE

GRAMMAR: Modifiers

1 Choose the correct options to complete the sentences.

1 I love Suzy's house! It's _____ beautiful.
   a quite   **b** really   **c** not very

2 I don't like that dress – it's _____ nice.
   a quite   **b** not at all   **c** very

3 'Do you like this music?' 'It's _____ good, but it's not my favourite.'
   a not very   **b** not at all   **c** quite

4 We don't want any dinner, thanks. We're _____ hungry.
   a really   **b** not very   **c** very

5 Everyone likes Laura. She's _____ friendly.
   a not very   **b** really   **c** quite

6 'Can you clean your bedroom? It's _____ tidy.'
   a not at all   **b** very   **c** really

7 'Can they speak English well?' 'They can speak it _____ well, but they want to get better.'
   a very   **b** not at all   **c** quite

8 She's _____ good at sport. She often wins competitions!
   a not at all   **b** not very   **c** very

2 Order the words to make sentences.

1 sunny / not / today / it's / at all
   _____

2 quite / good student / is / Emile / a
   _____

3 really / costumes / your / colourful / are
   _____

4 friendly / her uncle / very / is / not
   _____

5 goes / early / to bed / Paola / very
   _____

6 not / my / warm / are / gloves / at all
   _____

VOCABULARY: Places in a city

3 Order the letters to make words for places in a city.

1 QUESOM
   _____

2 TREHEAT
   _____

3 METNUNOM
   _____

4 HETACLADR
   _____

5 QERUAS
   _____

6 TRAPATEMN KLOCB
   _____

7 HRUCHC
   _____

8 NORETCC LALH
   _____

4 Complete the words.

1 My mum goes to the m_____t every morning to buy fruit and vegetables.

2 We live in an old city, so there aren't many s_____s or other tall buildings.

3 My sister loves reading. She's always at the l_____y in town.

4 There's a small s_____m here. They play rugby every weekend.

5 His brother-in-law's an accountant. He works in an o_____e b_____k.

6 In my village there's a b_____e over the river.

PRONUNCIATION: Sentence stress

5 ▶ 6.3 <u>Underline</u> the stressed words in the sentences. Listen, check and repeat.

1 That chair isn't very comfortable.

2 Her grandparents' house is quite modern.

3 It's a very famous painting.

4 That restaurant isn't at all expensive.

5 Our balcony is always really sunny.

6 This is quite a heavy table.

7 The restaurant is very traditional.

SKILLS 6D

WRITING: Topic sentences

A. _____ It's on the River Guadalquivir, but it's quite far from the sea. It's a busy and lively place with a population of 700,000.

B. _____ You can visit museums, art centres, cinemas and theatres. The Plaza de España is a very famous place. It was built in 1928 and is really popular with tourists. If you like being active, you can play football or golf at the parks and sports centres. There are lots of great places to go walking, too.

C. _____ There are really lovely restaurants where you can get delicious tapas and traditional Spanish food. You must try the delicious meat, Secreto Ibérico – it's fantastic!

D. _____ A lot of tourists come to the April Fair every spring. This celebration takes place next to the river – it's a wonderful party. There is horse-riding, music and women wearing colourful flamenco dresses.

E. _____ Nicer times to visit are spring and autumn, when it's sunny and a little bit cooler.

1 Read the text about Seville. Match paragraphs A–E with topic sentences 1–5.

1 If you visit Seville in the summer, it can be very hot. ____
2 Seville is also well known for its festivals. ____
3 You can always find something good to eat in this city. ____
4 Seville is a famous Spanish city. ____
5 There are so many things for tourists to see and do in Seville. ____

2 Complete each sentence about Rome with one word.

1 Rome is the _____ city of Italy.
2 More than 2.5 million people _____ there.
3 Walking is a great _____ to see the sights.
4 There are wonderful _____ of the city from the top of the Gianicolo hill.
5 If _____ like historical sights, go to the Colosseum.
6 There are also lots of really good _____ to eat.

3 Write about a city you know well. Begin each paragraph with a topic sentence. Include the following information:

Paragraph 1: Where is the city?
Paragraph 2: What can you do there?
Paragraph 3: What special events or festivals are there?
Paragraph 4: Where can you go to eat?
Paragraph 5: When is the best time to visit?

6 REVIEW and PRACTICE

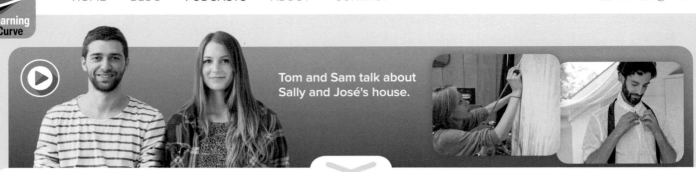

LISTENING

1 ▶ 6.4 Listen to the podcast about Sally and José's house. What is unusual about it?

a There is no furniture.
b There are two houses inside it.
c It's very untidy.

2 ▶ 6.4 Listen again. Are the sentences true (T) or false (F)?

1 Sally and José live in the country. ___
2 They don't like each other. ___
3 They can't live together. ___
4 Sally goes to bed late. ___
5 José gets up early. ___
6 They are both clean and tidy. ___
7 They have the same rooms. ___
8 José doesn't see Sally every day. ___

3 ▶ 6.4 Listen again and tick (✓) the parts of the house that Sally and José mention.

1 garden ___
2 dining room ___
3 kitchen ___
4 living room ___
5 bedroom ___
6 bathroom ___
7 basement ___
8 hall ___

READING

1 Read the blog on page 37 about Buenos Aires. Match paragraphs A–E with pictures 1–5.

1 ___
2 ___
3 ___
4 ___
5 ___

2 Choose the correct options to complete the sentences.

1 El Ateneo Grand Splendid doesn't sell
  a books.
  b furniture.
  c food and drink.
2 You can watch sport at
  a San Telmo.
  b La Poesía.
  c La Bombonera.
3 You don't have to pay for
  a the football matches.
  b the walking tours.
  c the coffee at La Poesía.
4 They sell cheap clothes
  a in the park.
  b next to the theatre.
  c at the market.
5 San Telmo has lots of
  a interesting buildings.
  b good places for music.
  c parks.
6 The Street art tour
  a is in one part of the city.
  b is in different parts of the city.
  c starts next to an ice-cream shop.

REVIEW and PRACTICE 6

HOME BLOG PODCASTS ABOUT CONTACT

Tom and Sam write about Buenos Aires.

The best of Buenos Aires

We asked our readers to tell us about their favourite places in the beautiful city of Buenos Aires. Thanks for all your great ideas. We want to go there – now! We hope you do too when you read our blog!

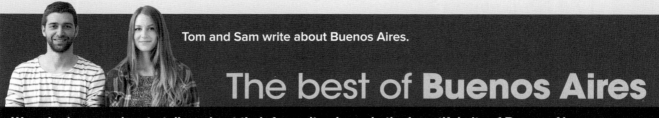

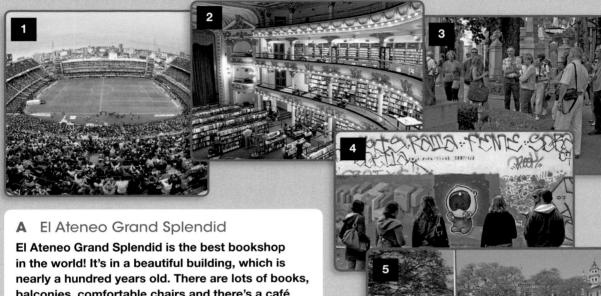

A El Ateneo Grand Splendid

El Ateneo Grand Splendid is the best bookshop in the world! It's in a beautiful building, which is nearly a hundred years old. There are lots of books, balconies, comfortable chairs and there's a café that sells excellent coffee and cakes. It's perfect for book lovers!

B La Bombonera

Above the houses and shops of La Boca you can find the football stadium. This is where the Boca Junior Football team plays. It's not too expensive to get a ticket for a match, and it's a really exciting place to spend some time.

C City walking tours

Every day there are free walking tours of Buenos Aires, and you can choose to see the city by day or by night. You'll visit modern and traditional buildings, from libraries to cathedrals. There is also a stop at the local market where you can buy clothes, food and drink – clothes are not at all expensive here. The tour begins in the park opposite the National Theatre and finishes in a bar where you can hear some live Argentinian music.

D San Telmo

San Telmo is the oldest part of the city. There are narrow streets full of interesting shops, monuments and some excellent restaurants, too. It's a great place to find an outdoor café, order a coffee and watch the world go past. A very popular café is La Poesía. It's next to a beautiful old church.

E Street art tour

Buenos Aires is famous for street art, and there are some really colourful paintings. The street art tour is a good way to learn about the artists of this amazing place. It takes you all over the city and finishes in a famous ice cream shop. The guides are really friendly too!

Our next blog post is about Egypt. Do you have any useful travel tips? Let us know!

37

UNIT 7 Food and drink

7A LANGUAGE

GRAMMAR: Countable and uncountable nouns + *some/any*

1 Are the nouns countable (C) or uncountable (U)?

1 cheese	C U	6 jewellery	C U
2 salt	C U	7 teacher	C U
3 library	C U	8 mirror	C U
4 bread	C U	9 pasta	C U
5 lemonade	C U	10 sofa	C U

2 Complete the sentences with *some* or *any*.

1 Is there _____ coffee in the cupboard?
2 Do you want _____ yoghurt?
3 There isn't _____ tea – can you buy some?
4 Do you have _____ onions? I need them to make lunch.
5 She usually has _____ fruit after dinner.
6 Would you like _____ tomato soup?
7 Are there _____ lemons in the kitchen?
8 Do you want _____ water?

VOCABULARY: Food and drink

3 Complete the conversation with the words in the box. There are two extra words.

> juice ice cream biscuits tea potatoes
> cake peas cereal orange mushroom

Miguel Peter's coming to dinner tonight.
Eva Great! I can make some
¹_____ soup. I know he likes it.
Miguel We've got some fish. Have we got any
²_____? I can make some chips. We can have some
³_____, too.
Eva That sounds good! What about drinks? Do we need some ⁴_____?
Miguel Yes, Peter's favourite is
⁵_____.
Eva OK. Now we need something for dessert. ⁶_____?
Miguel No, it's too cold! Why don't you get a
⁷_____?
Eva Great idea! And after that we can have
⁸_____ or coffee.

4 Write the words for the definitions 1–8. Then match 1–8 with pictures a–h.

1 a long green vegetable c_____
2 a small round red fruit s_____
3 you eat this in hot weather i___ c___
4 a long yellow fruit b_____
5 a long orange vegetable c_____
6 a large round green vegetable c_____
7 a small round fruit, sometimes green g_____
8 a round yellow fruit l_____

PRONUNCIATION: *some/any*

5 ▶7.1 Say the sentences. Are *some* and *any* stressed? Listen, check and repeat.

1 There are some bananas on the table.
2 Is there any milk in the fridge?
3 She's buying some strawberries at the market.
4 I don't want any biscuits, thanks.
5 There isn't any pepper.
6 I'd like some crisps with my lunch.

SKILLS 7B

READING: Skimming a text

BREAKFAST AROUND THE WORLD!

Breakfast is the most important meal of the day, because it gives us the energy we need to work and learn. In many European countries, the first meal of the day is a piece of bread and some coffee. In other countries, people eat much more. So, what exactly do people around the world have for breakfast?

Paulo, Brazil:
I have breakfast with my family – we sit together and talk about the day ahead. We usually have coffee and some bread with cheese. We also like to have some fruit – it's delicious!

Jason, Australia:
In Australia we have lots of excellent seasonal fruit, so it's a popular breakfast. I'm too busy to cook in the morning, so I often have an apple and some yoghurt. Sometimes I don't even have enough time to eat that, so I take it to work with me.

Jenny, Ireland:
I leave home early, so I rarely eat anything. I usually just have a cup of tea. I know it's really unhealthy! At weekends I have more time – so I have an egg sandwich.

Asil, Turkey:
My mum always makes my breakfast – she's an excellent cook. I usually have some bread, cheese, eggs and tomatoes – that's a popular breakfast in Turkey.

Yoko, Japan:
For breakfast, I often have rice and vegetables. Miso soup is a very popular breakfast in Japan, too. I sometimes have that because it's a healthy breakfast. It gives me energy to learn when I'm at college.

1 Skim the text. Answer the questions with one word.
1 Many European people drink coffee for _____.
2 _____ is Brazilian.
3 _____ is a popular breakfast in Australia.
4 Jenny usually has a cup of _____ for breakfast.
5 Asil's _____ is a really good cook.
6 People in _____ eat miso soup.

2 Choose the correct options to answer the questions.
1 Breakfast is important because
 a it gives you energy for the day.
 b you eat it with your family.
 c it helps you sleep better.
2 Paulo eats his first meal of the day
 a alone.
 b with his family.
 c with his friends.
3 Why doesn't Jenny eat breakfast?
 a She thinks it's unhealthy.
 b She's too busy.
 c She doesn't have enough money.
4 Jenny eats egg sandwiches
 a for lunch.
 b on Saturdays and Sundays.
 c every day.
5 In Turkey, a lot of people
 a don't eat breakfast.
 b eat the same breakfast as Asil.
 c drink tea for breakfast.
6 Yoko
 a has breakfast at college.
 b rarely eats miso soup.
 c doesn't eat the same breakfast every day.

3 Choose the correct options to complete the sentences.
1 Paulo eats breakfast with his family. *He / They / We* sit and talk about the day ahead.
2 Jason doesn't have time to eat breakfast. *His / Its / Their* morning is just too busy!
3 I love eggs. *It's / My / Their* favourite breakfast is an egg sandwich.
4 Fruit is really good in Australia. *Its / It's / It* a popular breakfast.
5 Asil's mother makes his breakfast. *She / Her / He* is an excellent cook.
6 Yoko thinks breakfast is important. *They / It / She* gives her energy to learn at college.
7 Most of us eat breakfast, but *you / we / it* eat different things in different countries.
8 We usually go out for lunch on a Sunday. *Your / Its / Our* favourite restaurant is Gino's.

7C LANGUAGE

GRAMMAR: Quantifiers: (how) much, (how) many, a lot of, a few, a little

1 Choose the correct options to complete the sentences.

1 I'm drinking ___ carrot juice at the moment. I want to be healthy.
   a much   b a lot of   c a few
2 Can I have ___ milk in my coffee, please?
   a many   b a few   c a little
3 How ___ meals do you usually eat?
   a many   b much   c few
4 Sara eats ___ cakes and biscuits. It's not at all healthy!
   a a little   b a few   c a lot of
5 'Are there any potatoes?' 'There are ___.'
   a a few   b a little   c much
6 Millie usually has ___ cereal for breakfast, but I don't think it's enough.
   a a little   b a lot of   c many
7 How ___ meat does he eat every week?
   a much   b little   c many

2 Complete the text with the correct quantifiers. Write one word in each space.

People often ask me how to stay healthy. I have a ¹_____ good ideas. Firstly, I always have a big breakfast, so I don't need ²_____ snacks in the middle of the morning. The people I work with eat a lot ³_____ cakes and biscuits at eleven o'clock – not me! I eat ⁴_____ little cake sometimes and a ⁵_____ crisps – but not many. How ⁶_____ cola do I drink? None! I only drink a ⁷_____ coffee, but I drink a ⁸_____ of water. And how ⁹_____ glasses of water do I drink? Probably about seven every day.

VOCABULARY: Containers and portions

3 Match the two parts of the sentences.

1 Could we have a can ___
2 I need a bottle of ___
3 Can you buy a box ___
4 Would he like a packet of ___
5 Is there a bag of ___
6 Laura has a bar ___
7 I often have a bowl ___

a of chocolate in her desk.
b water – I'm really thirsty!
c of pasta for my dinner.
d crisps with his lunch?
e of sweetcorn, please?
f onions in the kitchen?
g of cereal for breakfast tomorrow?

4 Complete the words.

1 I'm going to the shop for a c_____ of milk.
2 'There are no fresh tomatoes.' 'Why don't you buy some in a t_____?'
3 It's my birthday today! Have a s_____ of cake.
4 My mum has a c_____ of tea every morning.
5 It's really hot! Do you want a g_____ of cold water?
6 There are some olives in that j_____. Would you like some?
7 Have a p_____ of this cheese with your bread.

PRONUNCIATION: Weak form of

5 ▶ 7.2 Say the sentences. How do we say *of*? Listen, check and repeat.

1 I don't eat a lot of sweets.
2 How many cups of coffee do you drink?
3 Do you want a packet of biscuits?
4 How many glasses of juice do they want?
5 There is a tin of fruit on the table.
6 Where is the bottle of olive oil?

SKILLS 7D

SPEAKING: Asking politely for something

1 ▶ 7.3 Listen. What do the customers order at the restaurant? Choose the correct information.

1	2	3	4
3 customers Name: Cellini 2 x vegetable soup 1 x steak + chips 1 x lasagne 2 x mineral water 2 x fruit salad	2 customers Name: Cellini 2 x vegetable soup 1 x steak + chips 1 x lasagne 2 x mineral water	2 customers Name: Cellini 1 x vegetable soup 1 x lasagne 2 x steak + chips 2 x mineral water	2 customers Name: Cellini 1 x vegetable soup 1 x lasagne 2 x steak + chips 2 x mineral water 1 x ice cream

2 ▶ 7.3 Put the lines from the conversation in order. Then listen again and check.

a Are you ready to order your main courses? ___
b Can I take your name? ___
c The name's Cellini. ___
d Of course. I'll just go and get it for you. ___
e Would you like anything for dessert? ___
f Could we just have the bill, please? ___
g Hello, do you have a table for eight o'clock this evening, please? ___
h We have a table booked in the name of Cellini. ___
i For how many people? ___
j It's for two people. ___
k Hello, Giovanni's Restaurant. How can I help you? ___
l Can I get you any drinks? ___
m Ah yes, this way, please. ___
n Would you like a starter? ___

3 ▶ 7.4 Complete the sentences for asking politely. Then listen and check.

1 _____ both like the vegetable soup.
2 I'd _____ the steak and chips, please.
3 _____ I have the lasagne, please?
4 Can I _____ a glass of mineral water, please?

4 Practise saying the sentences in exercise 3. Make sure you use polite intonation.

5 Reply to the waiter's questions. Use the information in brackets.

1 Hello, Moonlight Restaurant. How can I help? (you/table/three people?)
2 Good evening, sir. Can I help you? (have/booked/name/Smith)
3 Would you like a starter? (like/chicken soup)
4 Are you ready to order your main courses? (can/have/large salad?)
5 What would you like to drink? (could/have/apple juice?)
6 Can I help you? (we/have/bill?)

41

7 REVIEW and PRACTICE

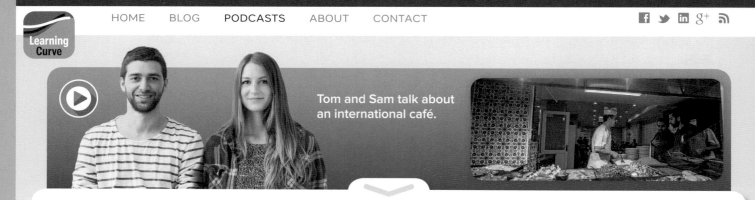

LISTENING

1 ▶ 7.5 Listen to the podcast about an international café. Number a–f in the order you hear them (1–6).

a peppers ____
b cheese ____
c rice ____
d tomatoes ____
e cake ____
f chicken ____

2 ▶ 7.5 Listen again. Are the sentences true (T) or false (F)?

1 Gabriela Romero is the manager of the international café. ____
2 People of different nationalities cook British food in the café. ____
3 The money from the café goes to charity. ____
4 Gabriela started the café alone. ____

3 ▶ 7.5 Listen again. Complete the sentences with one or two words.

1 Gabriela is from _____.
2 Gabriela lives in _____ now.
3 She made _____ burritos for her friends.
4 It costs £_____ to eat at the café.
5 Gabriela is making _____ for dinner.
6 The Turkish chef is making a big bowl of _____ pudding.

READING

1 Read the blog on page 43 about eating local food. Tick (✓) the things Alex eats during the five days he describes.

a mushrooms ____
b orange juice ____
c beans ____
d carrots ____
e cola ____
f tomatoes ____
g onions ____
h beef ____
i potatoes ____
j eggs ____

2 Choose the correct answers.

1 Why doesn't he eat much fruit?
   a They don't grow much fruit where he lives.
   b He doesn't really like it.
   c It's very expensive where he lives.
2 How does he feel at the start of the week?
   a He's excited – it's going to be fun.
   b He's not very excited – it won't be fun.
   c He's worried – he can't cook.
3 What does he eat on Day One?
   a nothing
   b porridge
   c supermarket cereal
4 Alex gets the ingredients for his omelette from
   a the supermarket.
   b the local shop.
   c his aunt's farm.
5 What happens when Alex goes to the local shop?
   a He doesn't buy the things he planned to buy.
   b He pays too much money.
   c He forgets his shopping.
6 What does Alex eat from his aunt's farm on Day Five?
   a peppers
   b beef
   c cabbage

REVIEW and PRACTICE 7

HOME   BLOG   PODCASTS   ABOUT   CONTACT

Guest blogger Jack writes about eating local food.

Going local

Did you realize that the fruit and vegetables you eat can travel thousands of miles around the world before they reach you – and could be weeks old? That's why many people are trying to eat locally instead. I asked Scottish teenager, Alex McKay, to try to eat only local food for five days. Read his diary to find out what happened!

Day One

The weather here is usually cold and rainy. We don't grow much fruit, so I'm not sure if this local only diet is going to be much fun!

For breakfast, I usually have a glass of orange juice and a bowl of supermarket cereal. Not today! I have some porridge (that's a kind of cereal that's popular in Scotland) and a cup of tea. The porridge tastes okay, and I find that I like knowing where my breakfast comes from.

Day Two

Today I go fishing in the river near my home. I'm really happy when (after a couple of hours) I catch a fish! I walk back and find a farm shop selling potatoes and beans. These will make a perfect dinner with my lovely fresh fish!

Day Three

I'm not sure what to eat today. Luckily, my aunt comes to visit. She has a farm and grows vegetables – she brings me some eggs, mushrooms and onions. Great – I have everything for an omelette. My aunt stays for dinner and we eat together. This is much better than supermarket shopping!

Day Four

Today it all goes a bit wrong! I go to the local shop to buy some carrots for a healthy soup. But I come out with a packet of biscuits, a slice of cake and two cans of cola. Not a healthy lunch.

Day Five

It's the last day! I cook some tasty beef stew with cabbage and peppers. The meat's from my aunt's farm, so I know it's fresh.

So how do I feel after my week of eating locally? Well, it can get a bit boring at times, but it's super healthy, and it's really good to know where your food comes from. Why not try it yourself?

UNIT 8 — In the past

8A LANGUAGE

GRAMMAR: Past simple of *be*, *there was*, *there were* and past simple: irregular verbs

1 Choose the correct options to complete the sentences.

1 _____ you good at sport when you were young?
   a Were b Was c Wasn't

2 We had a test yesterday. It _____ really difficult.
   a was b weren't c were

3 Last year I visited Rome. It's very beautiful, but it _____ cheap!
   a was b were c wasn't

4 Why _____ you at the party last night?
   a was b wasn't c weren't

5 His parents _____ rich, but they had a big house.
   a was b were c weren't

6 It was a warm day and there _____ lots of people in town.
   a was b were c wasn't

2 Complete the sentences with the past simple form of the verbs in brackets.

Last week, I ¹_____ (be) in New York. I ²_____ (go) with my family: my mum, aunt and two brothers. We ³_____ (have) a really good time. Of course, we ⁴_____ (see) all the sights – the Statue of Liberty, Central Park and Times Square – and I ⁵_____ (take) lots of photos. There are some great shops there, so I ⁶_____ (buy) lots of new clothes – jeans, trainers and tops. We all loved the food, too – we ⁷_____ (eat) some fantastic meals. We ⁸_____ (come) home on Friday – but I want to go back again very soon!

VOCABULARY: Inventions

3 Complete the sentences with the words in the box.

digital camera   toaster   smartphone
microwave   laptop   dishwasher   CD player

1 I couldn't live without my _____ in my pocket. I call my friends and play games on it, too!

2 We were late home, but mum left our dinner in the _____.

3 Our _____ is broken – the bread comes out black!

4 Suki's hobby is taking photos – she has a really expensive _____.

5 I don't enjoy washing up after meals. I wish we had a _____.

6 Do your parents still listen to music on a _____?

7 I couldn't do my homework last night. My _____ broke and I lost all my work!

4 Complete the conversation with the correct words.

Anna   What was there in your house when you were young, Grandma?

Grandma There wasn't a lot of technology in those days. For example, there was a radio, but we only had a black and white ¹_____ to watch in the evenings and we didn't have a DVD ²_____.

Anna   Really? And there was no ³_____ TV?

Grandma Oh no, only black and white! And we didn't have a fridge or ⁴_____ to keep our food cold, and there was no ⁵_____ dryer to dry your clothes when you washed them!

Anna   But were you happy?

Grandma Yes, I was! Life was interesting. We didn't have ⁶_____ in our cars, so when you went somewhere new, you sometimes got lost. That was an adventure!

PRONUNCIATION: *was* and *were*

5 ▶ 8.1 Underline the words you think will be stressed. Then say the sentences. Listen, check and repeat.

1 My grandmother's life was very interesting.
2 We weren't bored at school yesterday.
3 Her parents were both teachers.
4 There weren't many people in the market.
5 There was a bar of chocolate in the fridge.
6 I wasn't tired when I went to bed.
7 I told the waiter that my chips were cold.
8 It wasn't at all sunny last week.

SKILLS 8B

LISTENING: Listening for numbers, dates and prices

1 Order the letters to make life stages.

1 EB RONB
   _____

2 EVELA HLOOCS
   _____

3 OG TO SITYREVINU
   _____

4 TEG REDIRMA
   _____

5 EVAH A MAYFIL
   _____

6 TGE VDECRODI
   _____

7 TIREER
   _____

2 ▶ 8.2 Listen to the description of a woman's life. Write the numbers of the four life stages in exercise 1 that you hear.

___ ___ ___ ___

3 ▶ 8.2 Listen again. Complete the sentences with numbers, dates and prices.

1 Bertha wrote a book when she was ____ years old.
2 Bertha was born in ____.
3 Bertha and Fred had ____ children.
4 The camp was very popular in the ____.
5 Bertha cooked meals for ____ people every day.
6 British people could travel to Spain for just £____.
7 Fred died in ____.

4 Write the irregular past forms of the verbs from the audio.

1 begin _____
2 do   _____
3 go   _____
4 know   _____
5 leave _____
6 take   _____
7 think _____
8 meet   _____

5 Order the words to make set phrases.

1 now / for / bye
   _____!

2 of / would / cup / like / coffee / a / you
   _____?

3 do / you / do / what
   _____?

4 you / of / can / course
   _____!

5 just / time / I'm / in
   _____.

6 a / tea / cup / of
   _____

7 of / paper / piece / a
   _____

8 all / of / first
   _____

45

8C LANGUAGE

GRAMMAR: Past simple: regular verbs and past time expressions

1 Complete the time expressions with *last*, *ago*, *yesterday* or *in*.

1 _____ week
2 two days _____
3 _____ 1975
4 _____ afternoon
5 a year _____
6 _____ evening
7 _____ summer
8 three hours _____
9 _____ night
10 _____ the 21st century

2 Complete the sentences with the past simple form of regular verbs.

1 Where were you yesterday? I w_____ to see you.
2 It was a fantastic party! We d_____ all night.
3 We were friends when we were younger. We p_____ together every day.
4 'Did you have a good trip?' 'Yes, I really e_____ it, thanks.'
5 We p_____ a big party for Jen's birthday.
6 She s_____ really hard at school – that's why she has a good job now.
7 Sam t_____ to fix my bike, but it was no good – it was broken.
8 Diana o_____ the door and went inside, but no one was there.

3 Complete the conversations. Use the past simple form of the verbs in the box.

| want | use | not study | phone | enjoy |
| fail | not save | watch | stop | not like |

1 'What did you do yesterday evening?' 'Nothing much. We just _____ TV.'
2 'How was your Spanish course?' 'Terrible! I _____ so I _____ the exam!'
3 'What did you think of the new boss?' 'I really _____ her.'
4 'We _____ shopping online last month, but we _____ any money!'
5 'Were you busy last night? I _____ you but there was no answer.' 'I went swimming with my friend.'
6 'How was the film yesterday?' 'I really _____ it but Meg hated it!'
7 'Why did Emma leave?' 'I think she _____ to get home early.'
8 'This soup is horrible!' 'Yes, I think I _____ too much salt.'

4 Read the text and complete gaps 1–8 with one word.

I ¹t_____ to Mexico to see my sister, Emma, ²l_____ summer. She met a Mexican man a few years ³_____ and moved to Mexico to marry him ⁴_____ 2015. I had a great time there! I ⁵s_____ in my sister's apartment in Mexico City and we ⁶v_____ a lot of beautiful and interesting places together. She lives near a lot of good restaurants and cafés. We went out every night and I ⁷d_____ want to come home. ⁸Y_____ evening Emma phoned me. She wants me to go and visit her again next year!

PRONUNCIATION: *-ed* endings

5 ▶ 8.3 Circle the correct sound for the *-ed* endings. Listen, check and repeat.

1	We tried to tell you but you didn't listen.	/t/	/d/	/ɪd/
2	She decided to buy a new smartphone.	/t/	/d/	/ɪd/
3	They travelled across Africa by bicycle.	/t/	/d/	/ɪd/
4	Tom played with his toys in his bedroom.	/t/	/d/	/ɪd/
5	Katia liked reading books and listening to music.	/t/	/d/	/ɪd/
6	He waited all day to see her.	/t/	/d/	/ɪd/
7	Your mum looked very tired today.	/t/	/d/	/ɪd/
8	No one wanted to go clubbing.	/t/	/d/	/ɪd/
9	A police officer stopped the man's car.	/t/	/d/	/ɪd/
10	The bad weather ended in March.	/t/	/d/	/ɪd/

SKILLS 8D

WRITING: Planning and making notes

Last week, my date Carla invited me to go out. At first, I was excited, but I didn't have a good day.

¹_____, I went to buy Carla some flowers. ²_____ I paid for them, I walked to the cinema and waited outside. I waited there for almost two hours. When Carla arrived, she said, 'Sorry – my phone isn't working today!' I was a bit annoyed, but I didn't say anything. ³_____, we went into the cinema and watched a film. Carla laughed a lot. I don't know why, because it wasn't very funny.

⁴_____, in the evening, we went to a café. Carla ordered an expensive meal, but I wasn't hungry. We talked about the film and finished our food. ⁵_____, Carla looked in her bag and said, 'Sorry – I don't have any money with me!'

We said goodbye ⁶_____ I went home, but I was very tired and unhappy. I decided I don't want to see Carla again!

1 Read the text about Roberto's day. Look at the pictures and write a–f in the correct order.

1 ____
2 ____
3 ____
4 ____
5 ____
6 ____

2 Read the text again. Complete the gaps with the words in the box.

after   first   before   then (x2)   later

3 Answer the questions about Roberto's bad day.

1 When did it happen?
_____
2 How did Roberto feel at the start?
_____
3 What were the main events?
_____
4 How did Roberto feel after he said goodbye to Carla?
_____
5 What happened in the end?
_____

4 Write about a good or bad day you had. Use sequencers to show the order of events. Use the questions from exercise 3 to help you.

47

8 REVIEW and PRACTICE

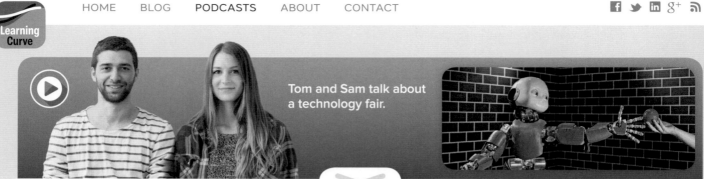

LISTENING

1 ▶ 8.4 Listen to the podcast about a technology fair. Which three inventions <u>don't</u> you hear?

a digital camera ____
b toaster ____
c smartphone ____
d freezer ____
e microwave ____
f tumble dryer ____

2 ▶ 8.4 Listen again. Choose the correct options to complete the sentences.

1 Izumi is an *inventor* / *a robot*.
2 Daichi is an *inventor* / *a robot*.
3 The robot can help *students* / *tourists*.

3 ▶ 8.4 Listen again. Complete the sentences with one or two words.

1 Tom was at the technology fair last _____.
2 Tom didn't buy a robot because it was very _____.
3 Daichi helps to guide people in big cities like _____.
4 The robot can show people how to _____ tickets for the subway.
5 Izumi studied technology _____.
6 It took Izumi _____ to make the robot.

READING

1 Read the blog on page 49 about a famous invention. Are the statements true (T) or false (F)?

1 Ruth Wakefield invented the chocolate chip cookie. ____
2 Ruth knew a lot about food and cooking. ____
3 The cookie's name comes from the name of a hotel. ____
4 She wrote a book about her life. ____
5 At first, Ruth didn't put any chocolate in the cookies. ____
6 When Ruth sold the recipe for the cookies, she made a lot of money. ____

2 Number the sentences a–h in the correct order (1–8).

a Ruth got married. ____
b World War II began. ____
c A business bought Ruth's cookie recipe. ____
d Ruth opened a hotel. ____
e Ruth left school. ____
f Ruth wrote a book about cooking. ____
g Ruth started her first job. ____
h Lots of people wrote to Ruth. ____

REVIEW and PRACTICE — 8

HOME　　BLOG　　PODCASTS　　ABOUT　　CONTACT

Guest blogger Penny writes about an interesting story.

A tasty invention!

You may eat chocolate chip cookies every day, but you probably don't know anything about the woman who invented them! Here's the true story of Ruth Wakefield …

Ruth Wakefield was born in Massachusetts in the United States on 17 June, 1903. She probably loved food from a young age, because it was very important to her when she was older.

After she left school, in 1924 she became a dietitian – someone who teaches people about food and how to eat healthily. In 1930 she bought a hotel called the Toll House Inn with her husband, Kenneth Donald Wakefield. It was very popular and visitors came from all over the world. One of the most famous visitors was John F. Kennedy, before he became the president of the USA in 1961!

Ruth became famous for her excellent fish dinners and desserts and in 1930 she wrote a very successful recipe book. Then, Ruth invented the chocolate chip cookie. It became really popular. Some people think that it was an accident and that Ruth wanted the chocolate to melt into the biscuit. But the chocolate stayed solid, and that was the start of the cookie we all know and love today! The first recipe for how to make this famous cookie appeared in Ruth's cookbook in 1938.

During the Second World War, families sent chocolate chip cookies to their sons, brothers and fathers who were soldiers a long way from home. They shared the cookies with other soldiers and so lots of people tried them and loved them. Ruth started to get hundreds of letters from people who liked her cookies and who wanted more.

In the end, Ruth sold her recipe for Toll House Chocolate Crunch Cookies to a big company. Ruth only got one dollar for the recipe, but she also got a supply of chocolate for her whole life!

Ruth died in 1977 aged 73. Next time you bite into one of her lovely cookies, stop and think about the person who invented it!

UNIT 9 Education, education!

9A LANGUAGE

GRAMMAR: Past simple: questions

1 Choose the correct options to complete the questions.

1 What subjects *was / did / were* he study at university?
2 *What / Who / Why* was your favourite subject?
3 *What / When / Why* did you do after school?
4 *When / What / Who* was your best friend?
5 *Did / Was / Were* she have a lot of friends at kindergarten?
6 *Who / How / Where* did you eat lunch every day?
7 *Were / Was / Did* there a library in your primary school?
8 *How / What / Where* did you do sport?
9 *Who / Where / How* was his first teacher at secondary school?
10 *Was / Did / Were* your teachers good?

2 Complete the conversation with past simple questions.

Sara	¹_____ were you yesterday? I phoned you three times.
Martin	I was with Peter.
Sara	Really? ² _____ did you do all day?
Martin	First we went to the park and later we played tennis.
Sara	And ³_____ did you go after that?
Martin	In the evening we went to the cinema.
Sara	Ah, you went to the cinema?
Martin	Yes, I ⁴_____.
Sara	⁵_____ did you go with? Your friend Lisa?
Martin	No, I ⁶_____. I told you, I went with Peter! What ⁷_____ you do all day?
Sara	Well, I tried to phone you. Then I phoned Peter.
Martin	Ah! ⁸_____ he there?
Sara	Yes, he ⁹_____. He was at home. So, was he with you?
Martin	Ah, no. He ¹⁰_____.

VOCABULARY: School subjects and education

3 Complete the text with the words in the box.

primary   nursery   homework   university
exams   secondary school

In Scotland, children usually start ¹_____ school when they are three years old. They spend two years there and then they go to ²_____ school when they are four or five. Here they learn to read and write. They don't take ³_____ – they play a lot and learn by doing things. They start ⁴_____ when they are twelve. They work quite hard and have to do more ⁵_____ after school. If they do well, when they leave school, students can go to ⁶_____ when they are about eighteen.

4 Complete the sentences.

1 I love learning about other countries so my favourite subject is G_____.
2 Ben hates M_____ because he isn't good with numbers.
3 Suki didn't study very hard so she f_____ her exam.
4 Which books are you studying in your L_____ class?
5 My little brother is only five so he goes to i_____ school.
6 Victor decided to study M_____ L_____. He wants to speak French and Russian.
7 We love sport so we always enjoy the P_____ E_____ class.
8 When I leave school I want to go to u_____.

PRONUNCIATION: Intonation in questions

5 ▶9.1 Read the questions. Do they have rising or falling intonation at the end? Listen, check and repeat.

1 Did you go to kindergarten?
2 Why didn't you study art?
3 Who was your best friend at school?
4 Was the lesson interesting?
5 Did you have homework at the weekend?

SKILLS **9B**

READING: Understanding words that you don't know

Meet three learners who found out that it is never too late to learn!

Francisco Pardo

My dad was a self-employed builder. He had his own business and wanted me to go and work with him, [1]_____ I left secondary school at sixteen. I didn't like working as a builder, though – I was bored, [2]_____ I started looking for something else. I bought a book about computer programming and read it from start to finish. Ten years later (and after a lot more reading and working with computers), I work for a computer company. I absolutely love it!

Bistra Nikolovo

I quite liked school, but I thought that when I left university that was the end of learning. Then I discovered online studying. Last year I took courses on Shakespeare, Italian and astronomy – I've always been interested in the stars! This year I'm doing Spanish and film-making. I don't want to stop [3]_____ I really enjoy learning this way!

Samantha Jones

I left school without any qualifications [4]_____ I had my daughter when I was eighteen. When she started secondary school, I found that it was really tough helping her with her Maths homework. I had to do something about it, [5]_____ I started a night class. My teacher was amazing, and I was really surprised that I could do the work. In the end, I went to college and studied teaching. I'm still doing that now – I work in a primary school.

1 Read the text and answer each question with a word, a name or a number.

1 What did Francisco study after he left school?
_____

2 What job did Francisco's father want him to do?
_____

3 Who is doing online courses? _____

4 Which language did Bistra study last year?
_____

5 How old was Samantha when she started a family?
_____

6 What is Samantha's job? _____

2 Complete 1–5 in the text with *because* or *so*.

3 Find the words in the text. Are they nouns (N), adjectives (A) or verbs (V)?

1 bored _____

2 discovered _____

3 astronomy _____

4 qualifications _____

5 tough _____

6 amazing _____

4 Match 1–6 in exercise 3 with meanings a–f.

a something you get when you pass an exam _____

b the study of the moon, stars, etc. _____

c not easy, difficult _____

d really good, surprising _____

e found out about _____

f not interested _____

9C LANGUAGE

GRAMMAR: Verb patterns: verb + *to* + infinitive

1 Complete the text with *to* + the verbs in the box. There are two extra verbs.

> do   travel   move   make
> become   start   get   study

> We're in our last year at school, and we're all planning what we want
> ¹_____ next year. Emile's family want ²_____ to Australia, so he's going to look for a job there. My friend Roberto hopes ³_____ a doctor after university. He needs ⁴_____ saving some money to pay for his course. And me? I'm intending ⁵_____ English so I can teach it one day. I'd like ⁶_____ around the world with this job.

2 Complete the sentences with *to* + infinitive or the *-ing* form of the verbs in brackets.

1 Do you like _____ in the sea? (swim)
2 We'd love _____ your new boyfriend! (meet)
3 Jack doesn't like _____ his parents' car. (drive)
4 William is learning _____ Japanese this year. (speak)
5 My uncle offered _____ us to the station. (take)
6 Would you like _____ in our new armchair? (sit)
7 They decided _____ married next year. (get)
8 Will he agree _____ you on Friday evening? (meet)
9 His dog loves _____ with a football in the park. (play)
10 Did Olivia choose _____ trainers or sandals? (wear)

VOCABULARY: Resolutions

3 Choose the correct options to complete the text.

> It's a new year and a new you! My name's Penelope Powers and I'm a life coach. Do you want to get fit and ¹_____ more exercise? I can help you with your goals – and if you want to ²_____ a marathon, I can make it happen! Perhaps you'd like more money? Do you want to ³_____ a car or your dream house? Or maybe you need to ⁴_____ a new job? I can give you lots of good ideas for when you ⁵_____ an interview. Of course, relationships are important, too. When you work hard, it's difficult to ⁶_____ someone new. I can help you ⁷_____ a relationship or ⁸_____ new friends. So, if you want to make a new start this year, let me know!

1	a be	b go	c do
2	a get	b run	c have
3	a buy	b make	c save
4	a be	b get	c earn
5	a have	b make	c save
6	a make	b meet	c join
7	a improve	b run	c have
8	a be	b make	c lose

4 Complete the sentences with the correct verbs.

1 Tony really needs to _____ fit. He drives everywhere and watches too much TV.
2 My boss isn't happy with me. She says I need to _____ more organized.
3 I love my job, but I'd like to _____ more money.
4 You don't need to _____ your diet. You drink lots of water and eat healthy food.
5 We need to _____ some money if we want to go on holiday to Greece.
6 She wants to _____ weight. Her clothes are too small.
7 Oskar's planning to _____ a gym next month.
8 My sister's a shop assistant, but she wants to _____ a new job as a receptionist.

PRONUNCIATION: *'d like* and *like*

5 ▶9.2 Say the sentences. How do we say *'d like* and *like*? Listen, check and repeat.

1 I'd like to go into town this afternoon.
2 They'd like to have a barbecue.
3 We like eating healthy food.
4 I like my new boss.
5 We'd like to speak Spanish.
6 They like keeping fit.

SKILLS 9D

SPEAKING: Sounding sympathetic

1 ▶9.3 Listen to the conversation between two friends. Are the statements true (T) or false (F)?

1 Rakeem has a lot of English homework. ____
2 He did an exam badly. ____
3 He wants to find a part-time job. ____
4 Rakeem needs some extra money. ____
5 He doesn't think it's a good idea to talk to his family. ____
6 He can't sleep because of his problems. ____
7 Talia thinks that the English teacher is a good person to ask for help. ____
8 Talia says that Rakeem needs to stay at home tonight. ____

2 ▶9.3 Order the words to make sentences from the conversation. Then listen again and check.

1 you / work / take / off / some / time / can
_____?
2 should / not / I'm / sure / I
_____.
3 don't / talk / with / why / you / your / family
_____?
4 good / that's / a / idea / really
_____.
5 visiting / tomorrow / about / the / how / teacher / English
_____?
6 do / let's / fun / tonight / something
_____!

3 Talia talks to Rakeem about a problem that she's having. Complete the conversation.

Rakeem	Is everything okay with you, Talia?
Talia	Yes, but my flatmate is very noisy. It's difficult to study there.
Rakeem	I'm sorry to hear that. ¹_____ you look for another flat?
Talia	I'm not sure I ²_____. It's expensive to change flats.
Rakeem	Why ³_____ you talk to your flatmate? Tell her that you need to study. I'm sure she'll try her best to be quieter.
Talia	That's a ⁴_____ idea.
Rakeem	How ⁵_____ studying when she isn't at home?
Talia	Yes, maybe. She isn't there this weekend! ⁶_____ have dinner at my flat tomorrow night.
Rakeem	That's a ⁷_____ idea!

4 Complete the phrases for sounding sympathetic.

1 Poor _____!
2 Oh no! I'm _____ to hear that!
3 That's a _____!
4 How _____!

5 ▶9.4 Listen to four situations. Respond using an expression from exercise 4. Sound sympathetic.

6 ▶9.5 Now listen to the situations again and write the response that you hear. Then listen again and repeat.

1 A My mum's really ill. She's in hospital.
B _____.
2 A I'm having a lot of problems with my boyfriend.
B _____.
3 A That Maths exam was awful. I'm sure I failed it.
B _____.
4 A I lost my wallet! And it had all my money in it.
B _____.

9 REVIEW and PRACTICE

LISTENING

1 ▶ 9.6 Listen to the podcast about Belinda's school days. Tick (✓) the subjects you hear.

a PE _____
b Music _____
c Maths _____
d History _____
e IT _____
f Modern Languages _____
g Literature _____
h Art _____
i Geography _____

2 ▶ 9.6 Listen again. Choose the correct options to answer the questions.

1 What kind of school did Belinda go to?
  a a school with no adults.
  b a school with no teachers.
2 Did Belinda like the school?
  a Yes, she was happy there.
  b No, she didn't like it.

3 ▶ 9.6 Listen again. Complete the sentences with one or two words.

1 Sam's favourite subjects were Music _____.
2 Belinda left school _____.
3 Now, she's studying Art and _____ at university.
4 The adults at the school helped the students with any _____.
5 At the start of the week, the students worked in _____.
6 Belinda often went on trips to the _____ and the _____.

READING

1 Read the blog on page 55 about someone who made a big change in his life. Number the sentences a–e in the order the things happened (1–5).

a Aapo met lots of new people. _____
b Aapo's friends gave him advice about how to be happier. _____
c Aapo found out about an ice climbing club. _____
d Aapo decided not to go to university. _____
e Aapo felt very unhappy with his life. _____

2 Use the information in the blog to answer the questions with one or two words.

1 How old was Aapo when he decided to make a change in his life?
  _____
2 Where did his friends tell him to go to do exercise? _____
3 What did Aapo see that sounded interesting?
  _____
4 What did Aapo decide to learn more about?
  _____
5 Which other activity is like ice climbing?
  _____
6 Where does Aapo live?
  _____
7 What must you do so that you don't fall when you're climbing?
  _____
8 What is different about Aapo's life now?
  _____

54

REVIEW and PRACTICE 9

HOME BLOG PODCASTS ABOUT CONTACT

Guest blogger Taylor hears from a young man about how he changed his life.

LIFE CHANGES

Do you feel you need to make some resolutions? Perhaps you want to change your life, but you're not sure how to go about it? Here's Aapo Virtanen's story. He wanted to get fit and lose weight and thanks to a new hobby, everything changed.

It was a few months before my nineteenth birthday. I lived at home, didn't have a girlfriend and I was overweight. School wasn't good either – I failed all my exams and I didn't have the grades I needed to get into university. Nothing was going right!

My friends told me I needed to change. They said, 'You should do more exercise and get fit. And you really need to lose weight! Why not go to the gym?' But I don't like going to the gym – I just find it really boring. I wanted to do something different, but I wasn't sure what. Then I saw a poster about an ice climbing club. I didn't know what ice climbing was, but it sounded interesting, so I decided to find out more. I phoned the contact person and went to the first meeting. That was the beginning of a new life for me.

Ice climbing is an extreme sport. It's similar to rock climbing, but the rocks you climb are icy! I live in the north of Finland, so in winter there is a lot of ice to climb. It's quite dangerous, of course, but I love it. When you are ice climbing, you can't think about anything else. If you don't think carefully about what you are doing, you could fall. It makes your brain feel really alive, too. And I've made some great new friends doing it.

A year later, everything has changed – and everything's better! I'm fitter, and I'm also quite slim. I now realize that university isn't for me. I want to get a job so that I can earn money. I need to save a few hundred euros so that I can train to be an ice climbing teacher. Then I can ice climb all day, every day!

UNIT 10 People

10A — LANGUAGE

GRAMMAR: Comparative adjectives

1 Complete the sentences with the comparative form of the adjectives in brackets.

1 My grandparents' house is _____ than ours. (big)

2 Sam was _____ than his older brother. (friendly)

3 This exercise is _____ than the last one. (easy)

4 Which is _____ – New York or Paris? (far)

5 These boots are _____ than your old ones. (nice)

6 Is the weather _____ in spring or autumn? (bad)

7 Walking in town is _____ than cycling. (safe)

8 The food in this café is _____ than my cooking! (good)

9 It was _____ yesterday than it is today. (hot)

10 The bus was _____ than the train. (fast)

2 Use the prompts to write sentences.

1 most shops / bit / expensive / the market

_____

2 London / much / crowded / my town

_____

3 the library / quiet / our classroom

_____

4 skiing / lot / dangerous / walking

_____!

5 the park / noisy / a nightclub

_____

6 your niece / clever / your nephew

_____?

VOCABULARY: Adjectives to describe places

3 Choose the correct options to complete the sentences.

1 We need to go shopping. The fridge and cupboards are _____!
   a safe   b crowded   c empty

2 I can't see anything at all outside. It's really _____.
   a ugly   b dark   c light

3 It can be _____ with so many fast cars on the road.
   a unfriendly   b lovely   c dangerous

4 Sasha didn't like her new school. Everyone was very _____.
   a beautiful   b unfriendly   c crowded

5 I made some vegetable soup yesterday, but it tasted _____!
   a horrible   b ugly   c dark

6 It was a _____ day so they decided to go to the beach.
   a friendly   b beautiful   c safe

4 Complete the sentences with adjectives with the opposite meaning.

1 Everyone loves Anna. She's a really *unfriendly* _____ girl.

2 Is it *dangerous* _____ to go out at night in your city?

3 Look at that building! Don't you think it's *beautiful* _____?

4 The streets in this town aren't very *dark* _____ at night.

5 I don't like catching the bus because it's always *empty* _____.

6 This pizza is really *horrible* _____. Would you like some?

PRONUNCIATION: *-er* endings

5 ▶ 10.1 Say the sentences. How do we say the comparative adjectives? Listen, check and repeat.

1 Her shoes were cheaper than mine.

2 The countryside is quieter than the town.

3 You're always busier than me!

4 Is your car safer than Alex's?

5 Anna was friendlier than her cousin.

6 Is Madrid bigger than Barcelona?

7 His hair was darker than yours.

8 It's noisier here than in class.

SKILLS 10B

LISTENING: Listening for detailed information (1)

1 ▶10.2 You will hear an interview about a model agency. Tick (✓) the words you think you'll hear. Then listen and check.

a elderly _____   e bald _____
b slim _____   f young _____
c tall _____   g overweight _____
d thin _____   h middle-aged _____

2 ▶10.2 Listen again. Write the words you hear instead of the underlined words.

1 He <u>owns</u> a model agency. _____
2 Their appearance is <u>very</u> different. _____
3 Many of us are <u>bored</u> of seeing beautiful models. _____
4 I <u>really liked</u> clothes and fashion. _____
5 Models don't always need to be <u>pretty</u>. _____
6 At first, it <u>wasn't easy</u>. _____

3 ▶10.2 Read the questions carefully. Then listen again and choose the correct answers.

1 When did Leon start his model agency business?
  a last year
  b five months ago
  c three years ago
2 What does Leon say about his models?
  a They don't look like most models.
  b They are all very beautiful.
  c They are all young.
3 Why didn't Leon become a model?
  a He didn't want to change his appearance.
  b He didn't like his hair.
  c He wanted a more traditional job.
4 What does Leon say is important for a model?
  a lots of clothes
  b a good appearance
  c their character
5 How successful is Leon's business?
  a It's not very successful at all.
  b It's doing better now.
  c It's changing all the time.

4 Order the letters to make appearance words.

1 D L N O B _____
2 U C Y L R _____
3 G R R E I N A _____
4 O S T H C M U E A _____
5 A F I R _____
6 M M D U I E - H E L N T G _____
7 Y G R E _____
8 A B E D R D E _____
9 N P G I I R C E _____
10 S S S G L A E _____

5 ▶10.3 Read the sentences and underline the words which you think have weak forms. Listen and check.

1 I mean, their appearance is quite different!
2 My models are very different from usual models.
3 What an interesting idea!
4 At first, it was difficult.
5 People like looking at my models.

57

10C LANGUAGE

GRAMMAR: Superlative adjectives

1 Complete the sentences with the superlative forms of the adjectives in the box.

> good bad big safe
> crowded old far friendly

1 This magazine says that _____ person in the country is 112!
2 Which is _____ star from Earth?
3 Alberto won a competition for _____ painting in the art class.
4 That's _____ cake in the shop! We only need a small one.
5 What's _____ city in Europe? I want to go travelling on my own.
6 I got _____ result in the test – I didn't get any answers right!
7 Mumbai is _____ city in India. About twenty million people live there.
8 Who is _____ teacher in your school?

2 Complete the text with the correct words.

I go to a photography club every Thursday and last week we had an end-of-year prize giving. Everybody likes Sara, so we decided she was the ¹_____ popular girl in the club. Ben is friends with everyone – so he got the prize for ²_____ nicest person. Lucy always takes fantastic pictures – she got the prize for the ³_____ photo. But Mara took the ⁴_____ exciting photo – it was of a car race. Her dad had the ⁵_____ car so he won. It was a great evening and I was really happy. In fact, I think it was one of the ⁶_____ days of my life!

VOCABULARY: Personality adjectives

3 Order the letters to make personality adjectives.
1 He is very **neitcdonf** in France because he speaks French well.
   _____
2 She's really **onersgue**. She always gets me a birthday present.
   _____
3 It is important to be **tolepi** by opening doors for people.
   _____
4 I like **relfhuec** people who smile a lot.
   _____
5 She is not very **kavtlieta**. I think she is shy.
   _____
6 My sister is really **vercel**. She passed all her exams.
   _____

4 Complete the personality adjectives.
1 Max can't swim so he was very b_____ to jump into the water.
2 We all laugh a lot when Wahid's here. He's a really f_____ student.
3 'Can I carry your bag for you?' 'Thanks, that's extremely k_____.'
4 Our cat's very l_____. It sleeps most of the day.
5 My sister isn't s_____ at all – she makes friends with everyone.
6 Everyone likes my Chemistry teacher, but my Music teacher isn't very p_____.

PRONUNCIATION: Superlative adjectives

5 ▶10.4 Say the sentences. How do we say the superlative adjectives? Listen, check and repeat.
1 What's the most exciting place in the world?
2 She's the kindest girl I know.
3 He is the laziest boy in the school.
4 Ella is the most popular girl in the club.
5 It's the funniest film of the year.
6 Who's the most relaxed person in your family?
7 Is she the most beautiful woman in the country?
8 My nicest present was this necklace.

Skills 10D

WRITING: Writing a description of a person

A WOMAN I ADMIRE

A Florence Nightingale was born in 1820 in Florence, Italy, but her family were British. After a year, they moved back to England. Later, Florence became a nurse and helped a lot of people. She was an attractive, slim woman with long brown hair and a lovely smile.

B Florence's parents wanted her to get married, but she decided to travel and to learn about the science of nursing. She was a nurse in hospitals in Turkey during the Crimean war against Russia. These hospitals were dangerous and very dirty and it was extremely difficult working there. Florence tried very hard to make the hospitals cleaner and safer places.

C I admire Florence Nightingale because she was strong and one of the bravest women at that time. Women usually stayed at home then, but Florence did what she thought was right. Her story inspired me and I want to be a nurse, too.

1 Read the text about Florence Nightingale. Which paragraphs give the information below? Write A, B or C.

1 why the writer admires her ____
2 facts about her life ____
3 where she came from ____
4 what she believed ____
5 what her job was ____
6 what she looked like ____

2 Complete the sentences about Florence Nightingale. Use a verb from the box in the past simple.

| travel | make | do | work | not be |
| be (x2) | not want | help | want | become |

1 Florence Nightingale _____ Italian but she _____ born in Italy.
2 She _____ to get married. She _____ a nurse instead.
3 She _____ to learn about nursing so she _____ to Turkey.
4 She _____ in hospitals in Turkey and tried to make them safer.
5 She _____ a lot of soldiers and _____ what she thought was right.
6 She _____ a brave and attractive woman and _____ a real difference to people's lives.

3 Join the sentences using a clause with *when*. Write two versions for each sentence.

Example
When she was young, she lived in Italy. / She lived in Italy when she was young.

1 Florence was a baby. That's when her family moved to England.
_____
_____

2 There was a war against Russia. At that time, Florence worked as a nurse.
_____
_____

3 Florence was young. At that time, women usually stayed at home.
_____
_____

4 Write a description of someone you admire. Include the information below:

Paragraph 1: Where is he/she from? What does he/she do? What does he/she look like?

Paragraph 2: What are the important events and achievements in his/her life?

Paragraph 3: Why do you admire this person?

59

10 REVIEW and PRACTICE

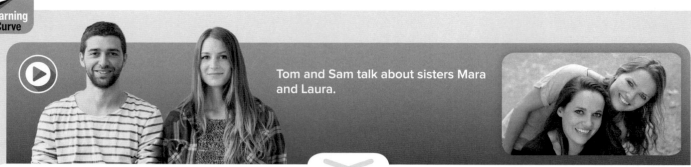

Tom and Sam talk about sisters Mara and Laura.

LISTENING

1 ▶ 10.5 Listen to the podcast about two sisters. Choose the correct answers.

1 What do Mara and Laura do?
   a Mara's a theatre director and Laura's an actress.
   b They're both actresses.
2 Do they have similar personalities and appearance?
   a Yes, they do.
   b No, they don't.

2 ▶ 10.5 Listen again. Are the sentences about Mara (M) or Laura (L)?

1 She was a quiet and polite child. ____
2 She's two years older than her sister. ____
3 She's tall and slim. ____
4 She has long, black hair. ____
5 She's a little overweight. ____
6 She has brown, curly hair. ____

3 ▶ 10.5 Listen again. Are the sentences true (T) or false (F)?

1 Mara works at a theatre in Madrid. ____
2 Laura is less famous than her sister. ____
3 Mara often has a lot of problems with Laura. ____
4 Mara often plays talkative or funny characters. ____
5 Mara prefers the parts that her sister plays. ____

READING

1 Read the blog on page 61 about some of the best places in the world to visit. What does the blog say? Choose the correct options to complete the sentences.

1 The best view is from the *Grand Canyon* / *Mount Ararat*.
2 Reykjavik is one of the *coldest* / *friendliest* cities.
3 The people in Auckland are very *kind* / *shy*.
4 Switzerland is the *most dangerous* / *safest* country.
5 Scottish people are the *funniest* / *most talkative*.

2 Complete the sentences with one or two words from the blog.

1 Mount Ararat is a very tall _____ in Turkey.
2 Readers decided that the _____ city in the world is Auckland.
3 One reader said that he/she talked to lots of _____ when he/she was in New Zealand.
4 The places which are safe to visit aren't always _____ as well.
5 A female traveller said she was happy walking in _____ of Switzerland at night.
6 Readers said that the Czech Republic, Denmark and Canada were also very _____ places.
7 The _____ food was the deep-fried bar of chocolate.

60

REVIEW and PRACTICE — 10

HOME BLOG PODCASTS ABOUT CONTACT

Tom and Sam look at the best and worst places to visit.

▶ You have your say

We all love travelling, but which are the best – and the worst – places to go to? Here are some of our readers' ideas. Do you agree with them?

◁ BEST VIEW

Many people think that the best view is the Grand Canyon in Arizona, but 60% of our readers say that Mount Ararat in Turkey is even more beautiful! This 5,000-metre-high volcano is an awesome sight – if you go there, take a picnic and make sure you have your camera with you!

◁ FRIENDLIEST CITY

We often think of cities as crowded places where people never stop to speak to each other. It doesn't have to be this way! Many of you voted for Reykjavik in Iceland. The weather may be cold, but the people are not unfriendly – lots of our readers wrote in to say how kind and welcoming people in this city are. However, in our readers' opinion, the people of Auckland, New Zealand are even happier to talk. One traveller said, 'I can't count the number of times strangers came up and started speaking to me. And on a three-week visit I got invited to dinner five times. Wow!'

◁ SAFEST COUNTRY FOR VISITORS

Sadly, some of the most exciting countries in the world can also be quite dangerous. But safe doesn't have to mean boring. Our readers voted the lovely mountainous Switzerland as the safest country to visit. One female traveller said, 'I feel totally safe walking around at night, even when it's dark and the streets are empty.' Sounds good to us! Denmark, Canada and the Czech Republic were also top of the safe places list.

◁ WORST NATIONAL DISH

We're sorry, Scotland, but the prize goes to you! Many people voted for your national sweet treat – the deep-fried chocolate bar. One reader said, 'This is the most horrible thing I have ever eaten! It made me feel bad for days afterwards.' We hope our Scottish readers don't feel too bad though – our readers also think you have the funniest people!

UNIT 11 On the move

11A LANGUAGE

GRAMMAR: have to/don't have to

1 Choose the correct options to complete the sentences.

1 She ____ save money because she's going to university next year.
   a have to   b don't have to   c has to

2 Do you ____ take the train or can you cycle?
   a have to   b have   c has to

3 He ____ go to work this morning.
   a have to   b doesn't have to   c don't have to

4 You ____ wash the dishes – I can do it.
   a don't have to   b have to   c has to

5 We ____ visit our grandfather tomorrow.
   a has to   b doesn't have to   c have to

6 I ____ have to go to bed early because it's Saturday!
   a has   b don't   c doesn't

7 She ____ do her homework before she can play online games.
   a has to   b have to   c don't have to

8 Are you coming to New Zealand? You ____ visit me!
   a doesn't have to   b has to   c have to

2 Complete the email with the correct form of *have to/don't have to*.

Dear Maria,

How are you? Dad and I are both well. Ella is working in a shop on Saturdays because she ¹_____ to save money to buy clothes! What is your house like? Is it near the university? Do you ²_____ to take the bus or can you walk? I hope you ³_____ have to get up too early in the morning! Are you eating well? Remember, it ⁴_____ have to be expensive to cook a delicious meal. I hope you can come home next weekend for your brother's birthday. So you don't ⁵_____ to do your washing this week, I can do it when you're here. What are you doing tomorrow? I ⁶_____ have to get up early, because it's Sunday. And your father? Yes, he ⁷_____, because he ⁸_____ walk the dog!

Love from Mum X

VOCABULARY: Travel and transport

3 Order the letters to make words for travel and transport.

1 The London **dguroudnner** _____ is often very crowded.
2 When my grandmother was 80, she had a ride in a **poctrelieh** _____.
3 You have to wear a helmet to travel by **toromkibe** _____.
4 Lots of people travel by **restoco** _____ in Italy.
5 Our **rryef** _____ takes five hours to cross the sea.
6 I prefer to travel by **cahoc** _____. It's cheap and relaxing.

4 Look at the pictures. Write the words.

1 _____   3 _____   5 _____
2 _____   4 _____   6 _____

PRONUNCIATION: have to/has to

5 ▶ 11.1 Say the sentences. How do we say *have to* and *has to*? Listen, check and repeat.

1 Does she have to speak English at work?
2 Do you have to go to bed early?
3 He doesn't have to cook this evening.
4 He has to finish his homework.
5 You have to visit me in Turkey.
6 I don't have to work tomorrow.

SKILLS 11B

READING: Reading for detail

Two friends, two different opinions ...

Best friends Cara and Vanessa went on holiday together for the first time this summer. Are they still friends? Read and find out!

Vanessa

I was so happy when Cara and I decided to go on holiday together this summer. Cara is my best friend, and I was really looking forward to it. In the end, though, it wasn't so great.

Cara is very energetic, but I like to relax on holiday. She wanted to take the train and go sightseeing in different towns and cities – but I wanted to stay on the beach! She said, 'You're on holiday! You have to see things! You can't just sleep all the time.'

We spent a lot of money on sightseeing and other activities. I don't think you have to spend money to have fun. Maybe Cara disagrees with that, though!

We will definitely stay friends, but we probably won't go on holiday together again.

Cara

Vanessa is a really great friend, and we had a wonderful holiday together. She was a bit tired sometimes – perhaps that was just because the weather was too hot.

We did so many fun things – we took a ferry to a little island, we walked for miles around beautiful countryside and I think we saw all the sights, too. One day we even did a parachute jump! That was certainly my favourite part of the trip.

Next summer, we're probably going on holiday together again. Possibly a sports holiday next time? I can't wait!

1 Look at the title and the pictures. What do you think the text is about?

a two friends who had a great holiday together
b two friends who don't feel the same about their holiday
c two friends who had a terrible holiday together

2 Read the questions and options. Complete the gaps with the words in the box. There are two extra words.

do   Cara   best   time   Vanessa   feel   money

1 How did Vanessa _____ before she went on holiday with Cara?
   a happy and excited
   b tired and sad
   c bored
2 What did Vanessa want to _____ on holiday?
   a go sightseeing
   b relax on the beach
   c travel on trains
3 Why did they spend a lot of _____?
   a Their hotel was expensive.
   b They ate in expensive restaurants.
   c They did a lot of sightseeing.
4 What did Cara like _____ about the trip?
   a the parachute jump
   b the weather
   c the ferry trip
5 What type of holiday does _____ want them to go on next year?
   a a beach holiday
   b a sports holiday
   c a shopping holiday

3 Now choose the correct options to answer the questions in exercise 2.

4 Order the words to make sentences.

1 go on holiday / I / with Vanessa / want to / next year / definitely
   _____.
2 prefers / holidays / maybe / relaxing / Vanessa
   _____.
3 spent / we / too / money / much / probably
   _____.
4 going on / sports holiday / a / next summer / possibly / we're
   _____.
5 enjoyed / her / my holiday / I / with / certainly
   _____.
6 our friend / is going / to come / next year / Mandy / perhaps
   _____.

11C LANGUAGE

GRAMMAR: *be going to* and future time expressions

1 Choose the correct options to complete the sentences.

1 *Are / Is / Am* your girlfriend going to come with us?
2 I *'m not / aren't / isn't* going to finish all these chips.
3 'Are you going to eat that slice of bread?' 'Yes, I *isn't / are / am*.'
4 They *isn't going / not going / aren't going* to stay in a hotel.
5 'Is he going to be late for class again?' 'No, he *isn't / aren't / is*.'
6 *Are / Is / Am* you going to buy some new clothes?
7 We *isn't going / are going / not going* to visit Paris this month.
8 'Are the children going to get dressed soon?' 'Yes, they *aren't / isn't / are*.'

2 Complete the text with the correct form of *going to*.

I'm really excited about my plans for the summer. First, I ¹_____ work for two weeks in a café. I ²_____ go out because I have to save money. After that, my cousin Kinga ³_____ come to visit me from Hungary. We ⁴_____ go travelling around Europe. I can't wait! Her parents ⁵_____ come to my house, too, but they ⁶_____ come travelling with us. Kinga and I ⁷_____ take the bus – the train is much faster. Where ⁸_____ stay? I don't know yet! But I know it ⁹_____ be anywhere expensive, because Kinga ¹⁰_____ have much money.

VOCABULARY: Holiday activities

3 Choose the correct options to complete the email.

Hi Carla,

I'm having a great time here in Crete! It's a really beautiful place. We're ¹____ in a hotel near the sea. You know I love relaxing on the ²____ or ³____ the pool, so this is perfect for me! We're here for ten days before we come home.

There's only one problem. Mum and dad want us to ⁴____ sightseeing and visit ⁵____. I don't want to! It's really hot and I don't enjoy looking at old buildings!

My brother Sam is having a lot of fun, too. He ⁶____ surfing every day, all day!

See you soon,
Daphne

1 a	staying	b	going	c	visiting
2 a	mountains	b	beach	c	surfing
3 a	by	b	on	c	to
4 a	be	b	get	c	go
5 a	campsites	b	museums	c	mountains
6 a	has	b	does	c	goes

4 Complete the sentences.

1 We went on h_____ to Wales. It rained every day!
2 I really want to go swimming. Can we go to the b_____ later?
3 In summer, I love sitting by the p_____ reading a book.
4 We enjoy walking so we're going t_____ in Argentina.
5 Where did you stay? Were you at a c_____?
6 Mario loves old paintings – he wants to v_____ an art gallery tomorrow.

PRONUNCIATION: Sentence stress

5 ▶11.2 Say the sentences. Listen and repeat.

1 I'm going to stay with friends.
2 We're going to be more organized.
3 You aren't going to run a marathon.
4 He isn't going to have an interview.
5 Is she going to swim with us?
6 Are you going to see Ernesto tonight?

SKILLS 11D

SPEAKING: Checking information

1 ▶11.3 Listen to the conversation at a hotel. Choose the correct answers.

1 Mr Gutierrez is staying at the Amberton Hotel for ___ nights.
   a three   b four   c five
2 He is staying on the ___ floor.
   a seventh   b eighth   c ninth
3 They serve breakfast from ___ in the morning.
   a seven   b eight   c nine

2 ▶11.3 Complete the conversation with the words in the box. Listen again and check.

spell   checking   password   sign   reservation
floor   booked   key   breakfast   ID

Receptionist	Good afternoon. Welcome to the Amberton Hotel. ¹_____ in?
Mr Gutierrez	Yes. I have a ²_____ under the name of Gutierrez.
Receptionist	Could you ³_____ your surname, please?
Mr Gutierrez	Yes, it's G-U-T-I-E-R-R-E-Z.
Receptionist	You're ⁴_____ for three nights and checking out on Friday. Is that correct?
Mr Gutierrez	Yes, that's right.
Receptionist	Ah, yes. Can I have your ⁵_____, please?
Mr Gutierrez	Yes, of course.
Receptionist	Can you ⁶_____ this form, please? OK. Here's your ⁷_____. You're on the ninth floor.
Mr Gutierrez	What's the Wi-Fi ⁸_____?
Receptionist	It's Amberton, the name of the hotel.
Mr Gutierrez	Great, thanks! And what time is ⁹_____?
Receptionist	It's from seven to nine.
Mr Gutierrez	Thank you. Which ¹⁰_____ did you say? The eighth?
Receptionist	The ninth. Enjoy your stay.
Mr Gutierrez	Thank you!

3 Complete the phrases to check information.

1 You're booked for six nights and checking out on Friday. Is that _____?
2 Thank you. My room's on the seventh floor, _____?
3 _____ you say breakfast's from half past eight?

4 Are the phrases in exercise 3 formal (F), neutral (N) or informal (I)?

1 _____
2 _____
3 _____

5 ▶11.4 Listen to five sentences. Who says them? Write receptionist (R) or guest (G).

1 _____
2 _____
3 _____
4 _____
5 _____

6 ▶11.4 Listen again. Respond and check the information with the receptionist or guest.

7 Read the situations and check the information. You are a guest. Use a formal (F), neutral (N) or informal (I) phrase.

1 **Receptionist** 'Dinner is from 7.30 p.m. to 9.45 p.m.' (N)
   _____
2 **You** 'The price for a double room is £75.' (F)
   _____
3 **You** 'There's Wi-Fi in every room.' (I)
   _____
4 **Receptionist** 'Your room is on the eleventh floor.' (N)
   _____
5 **You** 'There's a gym in the hotel.' (F)
   _____
6 **Receptionist** 'Breakfast isn't included in the price.' (N)
   _____

11 REVIEW and PRACTICE

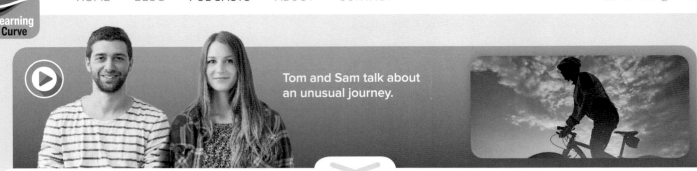

LISTENING

1 ▶ 11.5 Listen to the podcast about an unusual journey. Are the sentences about Ben true (T) or false (F)?

1 He finished his journey in the spring. ____
2 He is travelling to places that begin with the same letter. ____
3 He is planning to visit the beach. ____
4 He will go sightseeing in Bolivia. ____
5 He is going to Tokyo next year. ____

2 ▶ 11.5 Listen again. Choose the correct answers.

1 Where did Ben start his journey?
   a Belgium
   b Britain
   c Budapest
2 How is Ben going to travel to Bolivia?
   a by plane
   b by bike
   c by bus
3 Ben isn't working for ___ months.
   a three
   b four
   c six
4 What does Ben say is interesting about Bosnia?
   a its beaches
   b the history
   c everything
5 Where will Ben go surfing?
   a Bosnia
   b Belize
   c Bolivia
6 Which of the places <u>doesn't</u> Ben mention?
   a Toledo
   b Tokyo
   c Turkey

READING

1 Read the blog on page 67 about holiday jobs. Complete the sentences with *Kyra*, *Oliver* or *Stefano*.

1 _____ had a job working with old people.
2 _____ is going to teach children art.
3 _____ stayed at a campsite last year.
4 _____ went to the Mediterranean.
5 _____ worked in two different countries.
6 _____ likes working with children.

2 Are the sentences true (T), false (F) or doesn't say (DS)?

1 You need a lot of money to travel around the world. ____
2 You have to be fit to pick fruit. ____
3 Picking fruit is an easy job and it pays well. ____
4 Kyra ate a lot of fruit when she was in France. ____
5 You can do different kinds of jobs on a cruise ship. ____
6 Oliver didn't like working on a cruise ship. ____
7 The people working on a cruise ship have to be young. ____
8 You have to like children to work at some campsites. ____
9 Stefano is going to teach the children English. ____
10 At the holiday camp the children can go trekking. ____

REVIEW and PRACTICE 11

HOME BLOG PODCASTS ABOUT CONTACT

Guest blogger Penny writes about working in different countries.

Work your way around the world

Do you want to go travelling, but you've got no money? Don't worry! You don't have to be rich to see the world. There are lots of ways you can visit different countries and earn money at the same time. Here are some of my top ideas.

FRESH AIR AND FRUIT

This is a popular way for young people to travel the world. You can pick grapes in France, oranges in Spain and olives in Greece. You have to be fit and enjoy outdoor life, but it's good fun and you can make friends from lots of different countries. Kyra Scott travelled around Europe picking fruit last year: 'I started in the UK, where I picked strawberries. Then I went to France and picked peaches. It can be hard work and I didn't earn much money. But I made enough to pay for the campsite and to buy food. I also got as much fruit as I could eat – I don't think I ever want to see another strawberry!'

SAIL AWAY

Cruise ships take thousands of holidaymakers every year to some of the world's most beautiful towns and cities, so they're always looking for staff to wash dishes, serve food, or clean the cabins. You have to work long hours, but the pay can be pretty good. Oliver Baum worked on a cruise ship this summer, travelling around the Mediterranean: 'It was a brilliant experience. The guests were all quite old and they were mostly really polite and friendly. I really enjoyed looking after them!'

WORK AT A HOLIDAY CAMP

If you like working with other people, why not look for a job on a campsite? Holiday camps are always looking for young people to help with entertainment and activities. If you like children, this can be an excellent job. Stefano Rossi says: 'I'm going to work on a campsite in Spain next year. I'm going to look after children in the morning. They do painting and drama and lots of other activities, like surfing. You don't have to speak Spanish, as lots of the holidaymakers are English – but it helps if you do!'

You see? No money – no problem! Start making your travel plans now!

UNIT 12

Enjoy yourself

12A — LANGUAGE

GRAMMAR: Present perfect with *ever* and *never*

1 Order the words to make sentences and questions in the present perfect.

1 ever / you / the Northern Lights / seen / have

_____?

2 have / a blog / written / they / never

_____.

3 has / this book / read / he / ever

_____?

4 been / never / together / we've / bowling

_____.

5 ever / we / your sister-in-law / have / met

_____?

6 hasn't / karate / do / he / to / gone

_____.

2 Complete the conversation with the present perfect form of the verbs in brackets.

Marta I'm having a party on Saturday! Do you want to help? I need to be really organized!

Piotr ¹_____ (I/never/organize) a party before. But I'd love to help!

Marta Great, thanks. ²_____ (you/ever/make) pizza?

Piotr No, ³_____ (I/not)!

Marta That's OK. ⁴_____ (I/never/make) one either!

Piotr ⁵_____ (Sam/ever/cook) for a party? We could ask him.

Marta Great idea! ⁶_____ (he/have) lots of parties. ⁷_____ (I/go) to some of them.

Piotr But ⁸_____ (I/not/see) him this week. Is he at home?

Marta Oh no! I remember now. ⁹_____ (he/go) to visit his aunt and uncle in Germany! He comes back next week.

VOCABULARY: Entertainment

3 Complete the text with the words in the box. There is one extra word.

concerts   artist   singer   match   exhibition   bands   opera

Although my town is small, there's a lot to do. This weekend, I went to a really interesting art ¹_____ in the gallery near my house. I saw some beautiful paintings. I met the ²_____ and it was really interesting hearing him talk about his work. My town is also famous for music. There's a festival every year and many ³_____ from different countries come to play. There's a small jazz club near my house, too. It stays open late and has great ⁴_____! If you prefer classical music, you can see an ⁵_____. I love the music – when I was younger I wanted to be an opera ⁶_____. It didn't happen, but I still love watching and dreaming!

4 Complete the words.

1 We love films with Daniel Radcliffe. He's a brilliant a_____r.

2 The rugby p_____s were really happy when their team won.

3 I saw *Swan Lake* at the theatre last night. It's my favourite b_____t.

4 How many m_____s are in the band?

5 I don't mind watching baseball on TV, but I've never been to a m_____h.

6 There were two d_____s and a traditional Spanish guitarist in the show.

PRONUNCIATION: Sentence stress

5 ▶ 12.1 Say the sentences. Listen and repeat.

1 Have you ever been to this gallery?

2 I've never played the violin.

3 I've served food in a café.

4 Have you ever been to a rock concert?

5 I haven't tried Vietnamese food.

6 I haven't been to Canada.

7 I've been to Poland.

8 I've never written a song.

68

SKILLS 12B

LISTENING: Listening for detailed information (2)

1 ▶ 12.2 Listen to the conversation about birthdays. Which adjectives describe the things below?

1 Layla's last birthday — *amazing / fun / terrible*
2 Peter's last birthday — *boring / awesome / strange*
3 The ending of the play — *sad / interesting / exciting*
4 The Halloween costumes — *awful / scary / cool*

2 ▶ 12.2 Listen again. Choose the correct answers.

1 Who is Ben?
   a Layla's father
   b Layla's friend
   c Layla's cousin
2 How did Layla get to Paris?
   a by bus
   b by train
   c by car
3 Who took Peter to see a play?
   a his girlfriend
   b Layla
   c his best friend
4 When is Layla's birthday?
   a 29 October
   b 30 October
   c 31 October
5 What kind of party does Peter suggest?
   a a surprise party
   b a party with costumes
   c a strange party

3 Listen again. Answer the questions. Write complete sentences.

1 How many of Layla's friends and family were on the train to Paris?
   _____
2 How long did Layla and her friends and family go to Paris for?
   _____
3 What did Peter's girlfriend do after the play?
   _____
4 Has Layla had a costume party before?
   _____

4 ▶ 12.3 Read the sentences. Mark the links between words. Listen, check and repeat.

1 Last year I had an amazing birthday.
2 My cousin organized a surprise party for me.
3 I thought I was going to see an action film.
4 Everyone can get dressed up in scary costumes.
5 When I was eight years old.

12C LANGUAGE

GRAMMAR: Present perfect and past simple

1 Choose the correct options to complete the sentences.

1 We _____ Cara last night. She looked great.
   a have seen
   b saw

2 _____ a letter to a famous person?
   a Have you ever written
   b Did you ever write

3 Last week they _____ the new pizza restaurant.
   a tried
   b have tried

4 He _____ any of the *Harry Potter* films.
   a has never seen
   b never saw

5 When _____ to the gym?
   a have you been
   b did you go

6 She _____ her boyfriend at school.
   a met
   b has met

7 Where _____ that new watch?
   a have you bought
   b did you buy

8 'Has she ever been to Mexico?' 'No, she _____ .'
   a didn't
   b hasn't

9 How _____ in their exams last month?
   a did they do
   b have they done

10 'Have your grandparents ever used a smartphone?' 'No, they _____ .'
   a haven't
   b didn't

11 Who _____ at the party?
   a have you spoken to
   b did you speak to

12 They _____ to Brazil before.
   a have never been
   b have never gone

2 Complete the conversations. Use the past simple or present perfect form of the verbs in the box.

> not buy   drive   not eat   fly   go (x2)
> have   meet   not read   not see   speak

1 _____ you ever _____ in a helicopter?

2 I _____ you yesterday. I missed you!

3 I _____ any Russian novels. They're all so long!

4 Matt _____ never _____ sushi. He hates fish!

5 _____ ever _____ a dog?

6 Jan and Mo _____ shopping last weekend but they _____ anything.

7 _____ you _____ to the meeting or _____ you _____ by train?

8 I _____ never _____ to Sue. What's she like?

3 Complete the conversation with the present perfect or past simple form of the verbs in brackets.

Julia   ¹_____ camping, Matteo? (you/ever/go)

Matteo   Yes, I ²_____ last summer. (go)

Julia   And ³_____ you _____ it? (enjoy)

Matteo   It was awesome! ⁴_____ a brilliant time. (we/have)

Julia   Who ⁵_____ with? (you/go)

Matteo   I went with Sara and her family. ⁶_____ Sara? (you/meet)

Julia   No, I ⁷_____ (have). How long ⁸_____ for? (you/go)

Matteo   Five days. How about you? What ⁹_____ last summer? (you/do)

Julia   I ¹⁰_____ around the USA with my cousin. (travel) It was amazing!

PRONUNCIATION: Vowels

4 ▶12.4 Match the past participles that have the same vowel sound. Listen, check and repeat.

1 worn _____   a won
2 written _____   b spoken
3 drunk _____   c eaten
4 seen _____   d driven
5 flown _____   e met
6 read _____   f bought

SKILLS 12D

WRITING: Writing and replying to an invitation

Jan and Bob
are [1]_____

A HOUSEWARMING PARTY!

We'd love to welcome you to our new home.

Where: 12 Station Road

When: Saturday, 20 August at 8 p.m.

Children are welcome.

Hope you [2]_____ make it!

[3]_____: bob25@starmail.com

Toni Watts
To: ○ Bob White
Cc:

Hi Jan and Bob,

Thanks for the invitation. We'd love to [4]_____! It's a bit late for the children, but they can stay with their grandparents. We can't wait to see you!

Lots of love

Toni and Karl

Sally Evans
To: Bob White
Cc:

Hi Jan and Bob,

Thanks so much for the invitation. I'm really [5]_____, but I can't [6]_____ it because I'm going to a wedding. Hope you have a great time!

Keep in touch,

Sally XXX

1 Complete the invitations and replies with the words in the box.

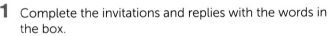

come   RSVP   sorry   make   having   can

2 Jan and Toni are talking on the phone. Complete their conversation with *a*, *an*, *the* or – (no article).

Jan	Hi Toni! Do you have [1]____ recipe for pizza?
Toni	Sure! Is it for [2]____ housewarming party on Saturday?
Jan	Yes – I love [3]____ pizza, but I don't have a recipe for it.
Toni	I can make some and bring it to your house before [4]____ party.
Jan	Really? That's so kind of you!
Toni	No problem. Where's your new house?
Jan	On Station Road. There's [5]____ bus stop outside. Thanks, Toni!

3 Reply to Jan and Bob's invitation. Use key phrases from exercise 1 and follow this structure:
- say hello
- say thanks
- decline the invitation
- say why
- say goodbye

4 Write an invitation to a party. Remember to include:
- the type of party
- the date and time
- your address
- other important information

71

12 REVIEW and PRACTICE

HOME   BLOG   PODCASTS   ABOUT   CONTACT

Tom and Sam talk about working in films.

LISTENING

1 ▶ 12.5 Listen to the podcast about a job working in films. Tick (✓) the adjectives you hear.

a brilliant ____
b cool ____
c exciting ____
d fun ____
e great ____
f amazing ____
g boring ____
h interesting ____

2 ▶ 12.5 Listen again and choose the correct options to complete the sentences.

1 What are 'extras' in a film?
  a They're the people in the background behind the actors. They don't speak.
  b They're the people behind the cameras. They help the film director.
2 Does Mikael like being an extra?
  a Yes, he does. He loves it.
  b He doesn't mind it but he says it's sometimes boring.

3 ▶ 12.5 Listen again. Are the sentences true (T) or false (F)?

1 Extras do the same thing every day. ____
2 They usually start work early in the morning. ____
3 They have to wait a lot. ____
4 Mikael doesn't like waiting. ____
5 He's met some famous people. ____
6 He was a teacher in a *Harry Potter* film. ____
7 He's also been an extra on TV. ____
8 He loves working in film studios. ____
9 He'd like to work in an office. ____

READING

1 Read the blog on page 73 about a singing group.

1 What kind of music does Ivor's group sing?
  a music for young people
  b opera music
  c popular music
2 Who is the group for?
  a unhappy people
  b people the same age as Ivor
  c people who have been to the opera a lot

2 Read the sentences. Are they true (T), false (F) or doesn't say (DS)?

1 Most teenagers like opera. ____
2 Ivor has sung in 50 different operas. ____
3 Reports show that singing makes people feel tired. ____
4 Lots of people want to join Ivor's opera group. ____
5 It is difficult to become a member of the group. ____
6 The group will only sing songs from popular operas. ____
7 The group doesn't make any money from singing. ____
8 Being in the group has helped some people's confidence. ____

3 Circle the opinion adjectives in the blog.

REVIEW and PRACTICE 12

HOME BLOG PODCASTS ABOUT CONTACT

Tom and Sam look at making singing fun.

Singing for fun

What do you think when you hear the word 'opera'? You might think 'boring'! It's true that opera isn't always popular with young people. Eighteen-year-old Ivor Golanski is trying to change that. In this special guest blog post, Ivor writes about his opera group 'Singing for fun'.

Many people my age have never been to the opera. I think that's sad and a little strange. I've been to about 50 operas in my life and every time has been an awesome experience. So I decided that I wanted to start my own opera group for young people.

I've read reports that show how singing together can help people who are feeling tired or unhappy. When you sing, the body produces special chemicals that make you feel happy and relaxed. Singing together is fun, because when there are a lot of voices, it doesn't matter if you sing a wrong note – no one will hear it and so you won't feel stupid!

You don't have to be a great singer to join my group – but of course you mustn't have a terrible voice! There are twenty members in the group now and that's growing all the time. We always have a good time when we meet. Everyone works really hard but we have a lot of fun together as well.

We've already played a few concerts, where we sang songs from some well-known operas that lots of people know and like. We've sung in schools, in the town hall and in our local theatre. We haven't travelled to any other town yet, but we'd like to. We're saving the money we make, and next year we'd like to go on a big tour.

Many people in the group tell me how singing has helped them in lots of ways. One member said, 'Before I joined the opera group, I'd never been on stage. It was too scary! I'd only ever sung in the shower and thought I probably had an awful voice. Now I feel much more confident about myself – my dream is to sing to a football stadium full of people!'

WRITING PRACTICE

WRITING: Opening and closing an informal email

Hello Bella,

How are you? I hope everything's okay in Italy.

It's nice to meet you. My name's Andreas and I'm eighteen years old. I'm from Germany, but I'm in the USA at the moment. I'm at a language school to learn English. It's great here, but I don't like the weather – it's very hot!

I speak English every day with my host family. My host mother is a doctor and she doesn't have a lot of free time. She has two sons: Andy and Greg. Greg is eighteen and Andy is sixteen. They are both students.

At the weekend we go shopping or we play sport. Sometimes we go to the cinema – there are some really good cinemas here.

Write soon with your news,

Andreas

1 Read Andreas's email to a penfriend. Complete the sentences.

1 Andreas is from _____.
2 He is eighteen _____ old.
3 At the moment, Andreas is in _____.
4 He _____ the weather there.
5 He _____ sport at the weekends.

2 Complete the sentences with *and*, *but* or *or*.

1 Andreas is German _____ he's eighteen.
2 Andreas can speak German _____ speak English.
3 He's from Germany _____ now he is in the USA.
4 He likes the USA _____ the weather is too hot.
5 He plays sport _____ he goes shopping at the weekend.

3 Are the words and phrases for opening (O) or closing (C) an informal email?

1 Hi   O   C
2 See you soon   O   C
3 Hey   O   C
4 Take care   O   C
5 Hello   O   C
6 Write soon   O   C

4 Write an email to a new friend.

- introduce yourself
- say your name, age and where you live
- use informal language to open and close your email

WRITING PRACTICE

WRITING: Describing a photo

Hi Malu,

How are you? How's your new job?

I know you like films, so I'm sending you some photos of me with my film group. We make films together on Tuesday and Friday evenings and we have a lot of fun. We sometimes go to the cinema, too!

Here's a photo of the film club at the cinema – we're watching a horror film! The second photo is of Ella and Sam. They're making a film in the park – it's a comedy film, so they're laughing. Sam is holding the camera in his hand. He makes great films.

See you soon,

Viktor

1 Read Viktor's email. In what order (1–4) does he do things a–d?

   a talk about the film group   _____
   b close the email   _____
   c describe some photos of the film group   _____
   d open the email   _____

2 Viktor has some more photos of the film club. Match the two parts of the sentences.

   1 In this photo I'm with _____   a and Sam with their cameras.
   2 Here's a photo of Ella _____   b my friend, Bruce.
   3 Here's a photo of _____   c sitting in the cinema together.
   4 In this photo we're _____   d my favourite camera.

3 Complete the sentences with the personal pronouns in the box.

| I   you   he   she   it   we   they |

   1 This is where the film club meets. _____'s a small café near our college.
   2 Ella works part time. _____'s a waitress in a café.
   3 Ella and Sam sing and make music. _____'re really good actors, too.
   4 I'm with Sam. _____'re talking about ideas for our next film.
   5 Sam has an older brother. _____'s at film school.
   6 What do you and your friends like doing? Do _____ enjoy watching films?
   7 This is my camera. _____ love making films with it!

4 Write an email to a friend about a free-time activity you enjoy. Use the notes to help you plan your email.

Paragraph 1: Ask your friend how he/she is.
Paragraph 2: Say what the activity is and why you like it.
Paragraph 3: Say when you do it and who with.
Paragraph 4: Describe two or three photos of your activity.

WRITING PRACTICE

WRITING: Topic sentences

Where to buy clothes in Paris

A _____ But where can you go to get the best clothes? It's easy when you know the city. Here are some of my favourite places.

B _____ There are lots of them in many parts of the city and you can find really interesting things. You can buy costumes and jewellery from the 1960s and 1970s – they're cheap, too.

C _____ On the Champs Élysées there are lots of small shops. You can buy beautiful shirts, trousers and jackets. Film stars and pop stars shop there, too!

D _____ The Centre Beaugrenelle is my favourite! It's a wonderful place to meet friends and to go for coffee, too. You can also go to the cinema there.

E _____ There are many great cafés and parks in Paris – you can always find somewhere to relax after shopping! Montmartre is a great area for restaurants!

1 Read the text about clothes shopping in Paris. Match topic sentences 1–6 with paragraphs A–E. There is one extra sentence.

1 If you like old clothes, go to the markets. _____
2 There are also a lot of big shopping centres. _____
3 The best time to go shopping in Paris is in spring. _____
4 Shopping can be hard work sometimes. _____
5 Everyone knows that Paris is a brilliant place for clothes shopping. _____
6 There are also some very expensive shops in Paris. _____

2 Choose the correct options to complete the sentences.

1 There are lots _____ good places to go shopping in my town.
   a on   b of   c at
2 The City Mall is a good place _____ fashionable clothes.
   a in   b of   c for
3 There are wonderful views of the city _____ the top floor of this shopping centre.
   a to   b from   c in
4 If you _____ to find some really different clothes, go to the Saturday market.
   a want   b try   c take
5 Eating at the View Café is a great _____ to finish the day after shopping.
   a time   b way   c part

3 Write a description of some different places to go shopping in your town or city. Begin each paragraph with a topic sentence.

Paragraph 1: Describe the locations.
Paragraph 2: Say what you can buy there.
Paragraph 3: Say when is the best time to visit them.
Paragraph 4: Say what you like about the places.

WRITING PRACTICE

WRITING: Planning and making notes

Last week I went for a meal with my boyfriend. ¹*Before / Then* we went, I was really happy because I knew the restaurant was expensive and fashionable. I got dressed in my best clothes: a beautiful white dress and my best jewellery. ²*Then / First*, my boyfriend came to meet me at my house. It was a warm, sunny evening and I felt brilliant.

Things didn't go well, though! The meal wasn't very good and we had a terrible evening. ³*After / First*, the mushroom soup was cold. ⁴*Then / Before*, we had fish with rice and salad. The salad was awful, too – I think it was a few days old.

⁵*Later / After* the meal, we had coffee. The waiter dropped a cup and coffee went all over my white dress. I was so angry! I ran out of the restaurant and went home.

⁶*Later / First*, my boyfriend called me. He was really sorry! He sent flowers and chocolates to my house the next day. We are still together, but I don't want to go back to that restaurant – not ever!

1 Read Sandra's story. Choose the correct options for 1–6.

2 Number a–f in the order the things happened (1–6).

   a The waiter spilt coffee over Sandra. _____
   b Sandra ate some fish. _____
   c The soup wasn't good. _____
   d Sandra's boyfriend invited her to go for dinner. _____
   e Sandra's boyfriend sent presents to her. _____
   f Sandra left the restaurant very quickly. _____

3 Read the sentences. Complete the summary of Sandra's story.
   1 The story happened _____ week.
   2 At the start of the story, Sandra's boyfriend met her at her _____.
   3 At first, Sandra was happy because the _____ was expensive and fashionable.
   4 The meal wasn't good because the soup was _____ and the _____ was old.
   5 After the meal, Sandra left quickly because she had _____ over her dress.
   6 Sandra and her boyfriend are still _____, but she doesn't want to go back to the restaurant again.

4 Think of a good or bad meal you ate. Write a story about it. Include the sequencers from exercise 1. Use the questions to make notes and plan your story.
   1 When did it happen?
   2 Where were you at the start?
   3 What were the main events?
   4 How did you feel at different times?
   5 What happened in the end?

WRITING PRACTICE

WRITING: Writing a description of a person

My favourite teacher is Mrs Young. She's my music teacher. ¹____ She has dark hair and happy eyes. She's always laughing! She's also a very good teacher and she loves helping people. Mrs Young lived with her aunt when she was a child. Her aunt was a musician and taught her to sing. Then, she learned to play the piano when she was three. ²____ She was a student at university. At that time, she met her music band, The Dots. She played with them for many years. She stopped playing with her band. After that, she became a music teacher. She loved teaching young people and she decided she wanted to teach music forever! She got a trumpet. After that, she started to play in a brass band. I admire Mrs Young because she is a very good musician and she works very hard. Her music classes are always fun. ³____

By Mia

1 Read the description of Mrs Young. Match the questions about her with notes a–e.

1 What does she teach? ____
2 What does she look like? ____
3 What did she learn to do when she was three years old? ____
4 Why does Mia admire her? ____
5 Why does Mia like her classes? ____

a always fun
b good musician, works hard
c to play the piano
d dark hair, happy eyes, always laughing
e music

2 Complete 1–3 in the description with the sentences. There is one extra sentence.

a I love singing and playing the guitar because she always teaches us that the most important thing is to enjoy music.
b She's a really friendly person and everyone likes her.
c Music is a very popular school subject in the UK.
d Later, she started to learn the guitar at primary school.

3 Join the sentences about Mrs Young using a clause with *when*. Write two versions for each sentence.

Example

Mrs Young lived with her aunt when she was a child./When she was a child, Mrs Young lived with her aunt.

1 She was a student at university. At that time, she met her music band, The Dots.
   _____

2 She stopped playing with her band. After that, she became a music teacher.
   _____

3 She got a trumpet. That's when she started to play in a brass band.
   _____

4 Write about a teacher you admire. Think about the questions below. Include two sentences with *when*.

1 What does this teacher teach?
2 What does he/she look like?
3 What do you know about his/her life and achievements?
4 Why do you admire this teacher?

WRITING PRACTICE

WRITING: Writing and replying to an invitation

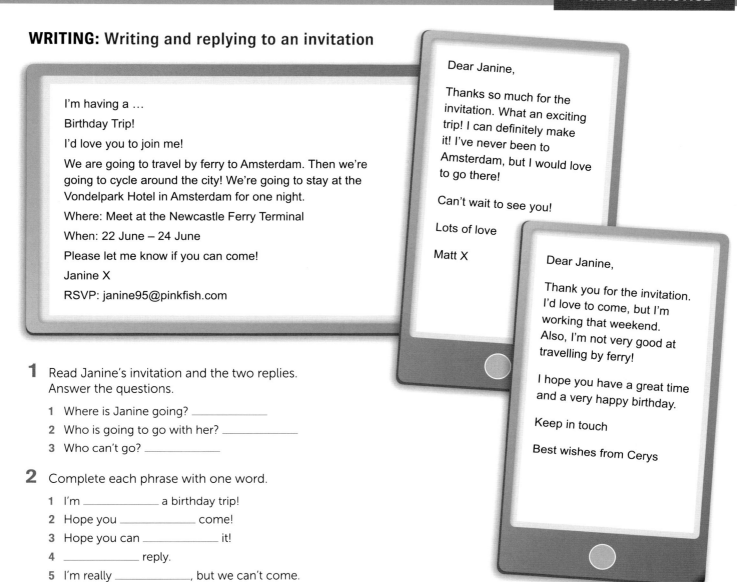

I'm having a …
Birthday Trip!
I'd love you to join me!
We are going to travel by ferry to Amsterdam. Then we're going to cycle around the city! We're going to stay at the Vondelpark Hotel in Amsterdam for one night.
Where: Meet at the Newcastle Ferry Terminal
When: 22 June – 24 June
Please let me know if you can come!
Janine X
RSVP: janine95@pinkfish.com

Dear Janine,

Thanks so much for the invitation. What an exciting trip! I can definitely make it! I've never been to Amsterdam, but I would love to go there!

Can't wait to see you!

Lots of love

Matt X

Dear Janine,

Thank you for the invitation. I'd love to come, but I'm working that weekend. Also, I'm not very good at travelling by ferry!

I hope you have a great time and a very happy birthday.

Keep in touch

Best wishes from Cerys

1 Read Janine's invitation and the two replies. Answer the questions.

1 Where is Janine going? _____
2 Who is going to go with her? _____
3 Who can't go? _____

2 Complete each phrase with one word.

1 I'm _____ a birthday trip!
2 Hope you _____ come!
3 Hope you can _____ it!
4 _____ reply.
5 I'm really _____, but we can't come.

3 Read Matt and Janine's online conversation. Choose the correct options to complete the sentences.

Matt	Hi Janine! I can't wait to go to Amsterdam.
Janine	I'm so happy you can come!
Matt	I'm going to bring some food for us to eat on the journey. Do you like ¹*a / – / the* chocolate?
Janine	I love it! Great idea. Thanks, Matt.
Matt	Is there ²*a / – / the* train to the ferry terminal?
Janine	No, there isn't. There's ³*a / – / the* bus at 2.30 p.m. though. I'm taking that.
Matt	Great! See you on ⁴*a / – / the* bus, then! Bye!

4 Reply to Janine's invitation. Use key phrases from exercises 1 and 2.

5 Imagine you are having a birthday trip. Answer the questions below. Then write an invitation to Janine. Remember to use key phrases from exercises 1 and 2.

- Where are you going to go?
- When are you going to go?
- How are you going to travel?
- Where are you going to stay?

Ⓡ Richmond

58 St Aldates
Oxford
OX1 1ST
United Kingdom

Printed in Brazil
ISBN: 978-84-668-2093-6
CP: 641564
DL: M-10055-2017

© Richmond / Santillana Global S.L. 2017
Reprinted, 2023

All rights reserved. No part of this book may be reproduced, stored in a retrieval system or transmitted in any form by any means, electronic, mechanical, photocopying, recording or otherwise, without the prior permission in writing of the Publisher.

Publishing Director: Deborah Tricker
Publisher: Luke Baxter
Editor: Helen Wendholt
Proofreaders: Amanda Leigh and Tas Cooper
Design Manager: Lorna Heaslip
Cover Design: Richmond
Design & Layout: Lorna Heaslip, Oliver Hutton
Photo Researcher: Magdalena Mayo
Audio production: TEFL Audio

Illustrators:
Simon Clare

Photos:
J. Lucas; M. Sánchez; Prats i Camps; 123RF; ALAMY/ Blend Images, INTERFOTO, REUTERS, Keith Homan, MBI, imageBROKER, Jose Luis Suerte, Harold Smith, Ian Allenden, Peter Horree, MS Bretherton, Pulsar Images, andy lane, Nano Calvo, Radharc Images, Westend61 GmbH, Colin Underhill, Gianni Muratore, Mary Evans Picture Library, Michael Wheatley, Alibi Productions, a-plus image bank, ONOKY - Photononstop, Directphoto Collection, Arterra Picture Library, Martin Thomas Photography, Agencja Fotograficzna Caro, Cathy Topping, Blend Images - BUILT Content, Geraint Lewis; GETTY IMAGES SALES SPAIN/ Thinkstock; I. PREYSLER; ISTOCKPHOTO/Getty Images Sales Spain; SHUTTERSTOCK; SHUTTERSTOCK NETHERLANDS,B.V.; SOUTHWEST NEWS/Leicester Mercury; ARCHIVO SANTILLANA

Cover Photo: istockphoto/wundervisuals

We would like to thank the following reviewers for their valuable feedback which has made Personal Best possible. We extend our thanks to the many teachers and students not mentioned here.
Brad Bawtinheimer, Manuel Hidalgo, Paulo Dantas, Diana Bermúdez, Laura Gutiérrez, Hardy Griffin, Angi Conti, Christopher Morabito, Hande Kokce, Jorge Lobato, Leonardo Mercato, Mercilinda Ortiz, Wendy López

The Publisher has made every effort to trace the owner of copyright material; however, the Publisher will correct any involuntary omission at the earliest opportunity.

Código do livro: 290520936
Lote: 795.080
Gráfica: Printi